Chicago

Seeing and Photographing the Windy City

Steve Geer

AMERICA
—
THROUGH
—
TIME

AMERICA THROUGH TIME®
An imprint of SUTTON PUBLISHING INC
www.through-time.com

First published 2026
Copyright © Steve Geer 2026

ISBN 978-1-63499-622-8

Typeset in Gotham
Printed and bound in the United States of America

Contents

Introduction

Chicago is one of the most photogenic cities in North America. Each year millions of visitors travel to downtown Chicago for work or play. Many of these visitors come armed with a camera and are eager to take pictures that show where they've been and what they've seen. There are spectacular standard views that can be recorded by visiting the top ten or twenty locations in the city. Guidebooks and travel posters suggest where to go and what to photograph. If you enjoy taking photographs this is great, but better still is to see the city with fresh eyes and take photographs that show things beyond the guidebook images. Largely avoiding the standard views, the images in this book show one photographer's take on Chicago in the twenty-first century. The photographs span the period from 2014 to 2025. The book is organized in sections with text at the beginning of each to provide a short introduction that includes tips for pursuing various types of photography in the city.

To provide a context for the images it is useful to know some of Chicago's history. Why is the city located at the southern end of Lake Michigan and how did it come to be the way it is? Chicago started life as a trading settlement near the mouth of a slow-flowing river. This was a marshy area located not far from a long-established portage between Lake Michigan and the Mississippi River watershed. In 1674 explorer Louis Joliet proposed a canal that would replace the portage and open a continuous water route between Lake Michigan and the Mississippi. It was the dream of this canal and its realization that drove much of the early growth of Chicago.

The town of Chicago was founded in 1833. With a population of 200 it was very far from being one of the great architectural cities of the World. However, within seven years its population had grown to 4,000. Along the way, in 1836, construction of the long-dreamt-of Illinois and Michigan Canal began. To pay for the canal, the state of Illinois charged three men, Hubbard, Thornton and Archer, to sell off unsettled parcels of land. With great foresight, they refused to sell the lakefront and declared it to be: "Public ground – A common to remain Forever Open, Clear and Free of any Buildings, or Other Obstructions whatever." In 1837 Chicago was incorporated as a city. The canal was completed in 1848 and in the same year the city's first major railway, the Galena and Chicago Union Railroad, was established. The stage was set for the city to become a major distribution hub and industrial center serving a vast agricultural region. The subsequent population growth was explosive. In 1850 there were 30,000 souls in the city, and by 1870 this had grown to almost 300,000. In addition, prolific railroad construction during the 1850s contributed significantly to Chicago's economic development and made it reputedly the "Railroad Capital of the World."

It might also have been said that Chicago was the "Mud Capital of the World." In her memoir Mrs. Joseph Frederick Ward recalled, "The streets of the young city were frightful, with deep mud and holes and many places marked 'No bottom.'" This was more than just an inconvenience. Given the city's topography, it was impossible to separate drinking water from sewage. *The Tribune* reported that in 1854 alone, cholera killed 1,424 Chicagoans. The solution was to raise the city streets by up to 14 feet. In the 1850s and 1860s buildings of five and six stories were raised using a system of screw jacks. In 1859, *The Tribune* reported: "Within the past year from fifty to sixty brick stores, in blocks of two to five to seven in number, have been thus raised." The result of this monumental decades-long endeavor was not only a city raised out of the mud but also the first city in North America with a comprehensive sewer system. Mud was not the only challenge for the growing city. The lakeshore south of the river was eroding and during every big storm Michigan Avenue was flooded. Chicago needed a breakwater, but how could the city pay for it? In 1851 the new Illinois Central Railroad offered to construct the much-needed Michigan Avenue breakwater in return for the public lakeshore. The city council passed an ordinance giving the railroad a 300-foot-wide strip on the lake and permission to build a trestle that would support double tracks. Thus, the city got its breakwater, but the "Open, Clear and Free" lakefront was, at least temporarily, compromised. In time the water between the railroad and the lakeshore became a stagnant lagoon.

At the heart of the young city was the central business area known today as the Loop. Bounded to the north and west by the river, and the east by Lake Michigan, the Loop is surrounded on three sides by water. This did not save it from disaster in the fateful year of 1871, the year of the Great Chicago Fire. The fire started west of the Loop, jumped the river, consumed the Loop, jumped the river again and headed north. When the flames died down 17,450 buildings were gone from an area covering 3.5 square miles. One-third of the city lay in ruins and nearly 100,000 people were homeless. However, Chicago's industry was largely untouched. It is said that reconstruction began before the ashes had cooled. The vast rebuilding program attracted talented architects from the east and Chicago was eager to reinvent itself.

Some of the rubble from the Great Chicago Fire was used to fill the stagnant lagoon created by the offshore Illinois Central Railroad. This extended Lake Park, the public land east of Michigan Avenue. In 1896 the city began extending the park into the lake with landfill beyond the railway, and in 1901 the park was renamed Grant Park. The lakefront could once again become "Open, Clear and Free." The lakeshore was also changing north of the river. In 1886 a broken-down steamboat, the *Reutan*, ran aground on a sandbar 450 feet from the shore. After several stormy days more sand built up around the wreck to form a small island. The steamboat's captain, George Wellington Streeter, saw an opportunity. He built a makeshift causeway to the shore resulting in more sand build-up, and then invited building contractors to dump on the sands. He would create his own city in the lake and claim squatter's rights. It took the authorities until 1918 to evict Captain Streeter for good. The new land built on landfill north of the river is the modern-day Streeterville.

Skyscrapers did not immediately rise from the ashes of the 1871 fire, but in the 1880s the price of land in the Loop increased seven-fold, providing a strong incentive to build taller. Which building we call the first skyscraper depends on our definition of skyscraper. If you are a Chicagoan, it was the Home Insurance Building constructed in the Loop 1884–1885 (demolished 1931). At ten stories it was not much of a skyscraper, but its technology opened the way for taller and taller buildings and Chicago became a city of skyscrapers.

In the nineteenth century, the development of Chicago had been vigorous and its population growth explosive, but there had been no overall plan to guide the city's evolution. Much of Chicago had become smokey, ugly, and unpleasant, traffic was chaotic, and railroad tracks isolated much of the city south of the river. After the 1893 World's Columbian Exposition in Chicago, architect Daniel H. Burnham presented plans for improving the lakefront. In 1906 the Merchants Club retained Burnham to make a plan for Chicago. The resulting document, co-authored by Burnham and Edward H. Bennett, was completed in 1909. It was a landmark in the new discipline of urban planning. The plan recommended improvements to the lakefront, the creation of a system of highways outside of the city, the improvement of railway terminals, the creation of an outer park system, a systematic arrangement of city streets, and the development of centers of intellectual life and civic development. Although not all recommendations were implemented, many were and the vision the plan presented has inspired the development of the modern city.

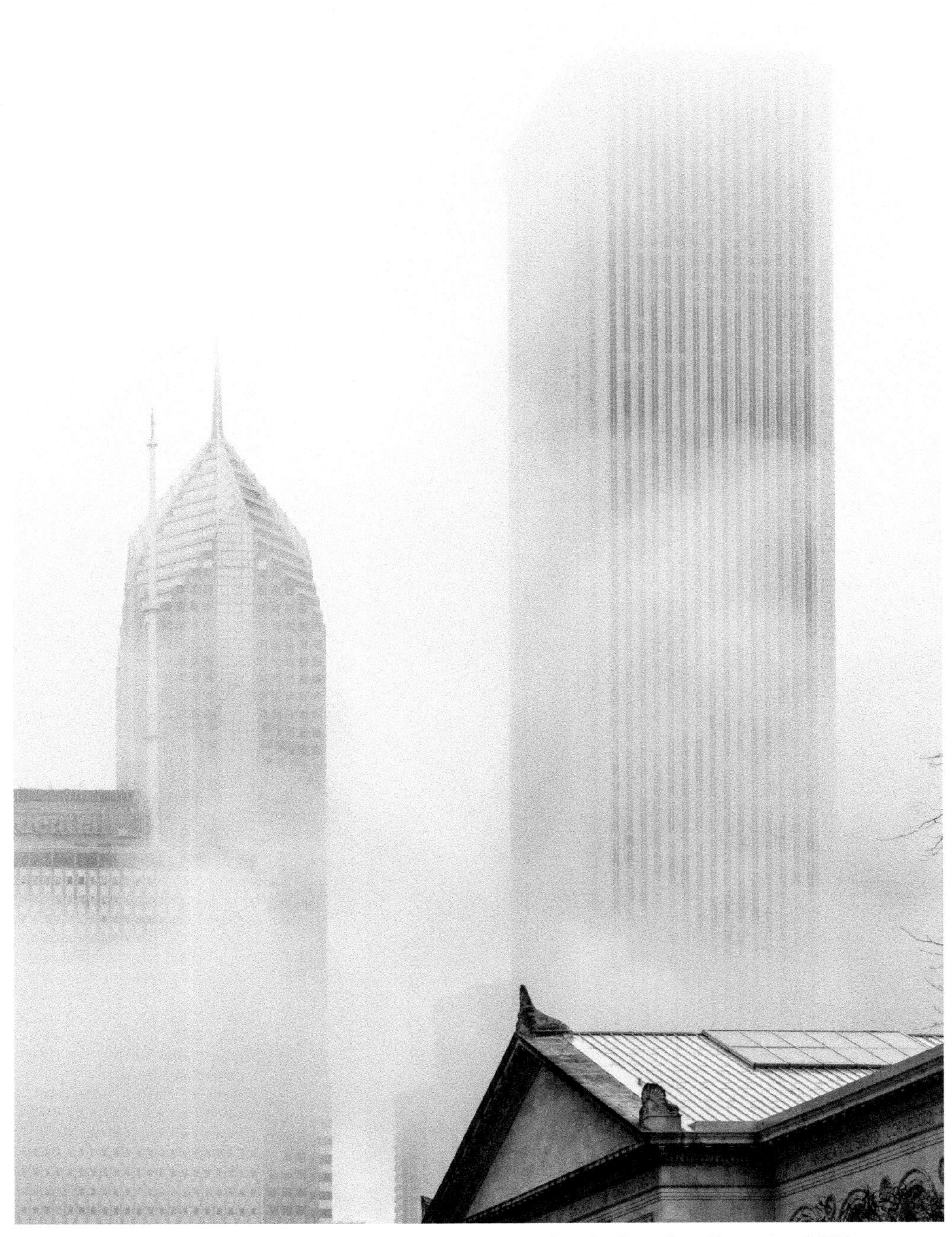

Lake mist drifting across the Aon Center and Prudential Plaza in Lakeshore East. December 2023.

1
The Loop

The Loop is the beating heart of the city. It originally derived its name from a cable carline that circled the business district in the 1880s. Later, this was replaced by the elevated railway. The Loop covers a large but walkable area. To navigate, it's handy to know that the streets are organized in a north-south and east-west grid with eight city blocks to a mile. Blocks are numbered outwards from the intersection of State and Madison Streets, with block numbers increasing in increments of 100. Thus, 800 S. Michigan Avenue is eight blocks, and hence 1 mile, to the south of Madison Street, and 400 W. Jackson Boulevard is a half mile west of State Street. For rainy days there is the Pedway, an underground system of walkways connecting some of the parking lots, stores, and government buildings. State Street is the main shopping street. The pandemic of 2020–2023 resulted in some empty stores. Nevertheless, during store hours the street bustles with people. The main financial district is along LaSalle Street which, lined with skyscrapers, has been nicknamed "The Canyon." Indeed, the entire Loop is a forest of skyscrapers with ages and styles spanning skyscraper history. The Loop also hosts the main centers of government. Each cluster of government buildings is adjacent to a plaza (Federal Plaza, Daley Plaza, and the Plaza next to the Thompson Center), with each plaza featuring an iconic sculpture.

Photographer Tips

i) Don't forget to look upwards. Skyscraper reflections can produce striking images.
ii) Early morning mist can drift in from the lake, especially in the Lakeshore East part of the Loop. This can facilitate atmospheric shots and minimalistic photography.
iii) Many building foyers are interesting. The Chicago Architecture Center offers walking tours taking you into some of the most historically notable.

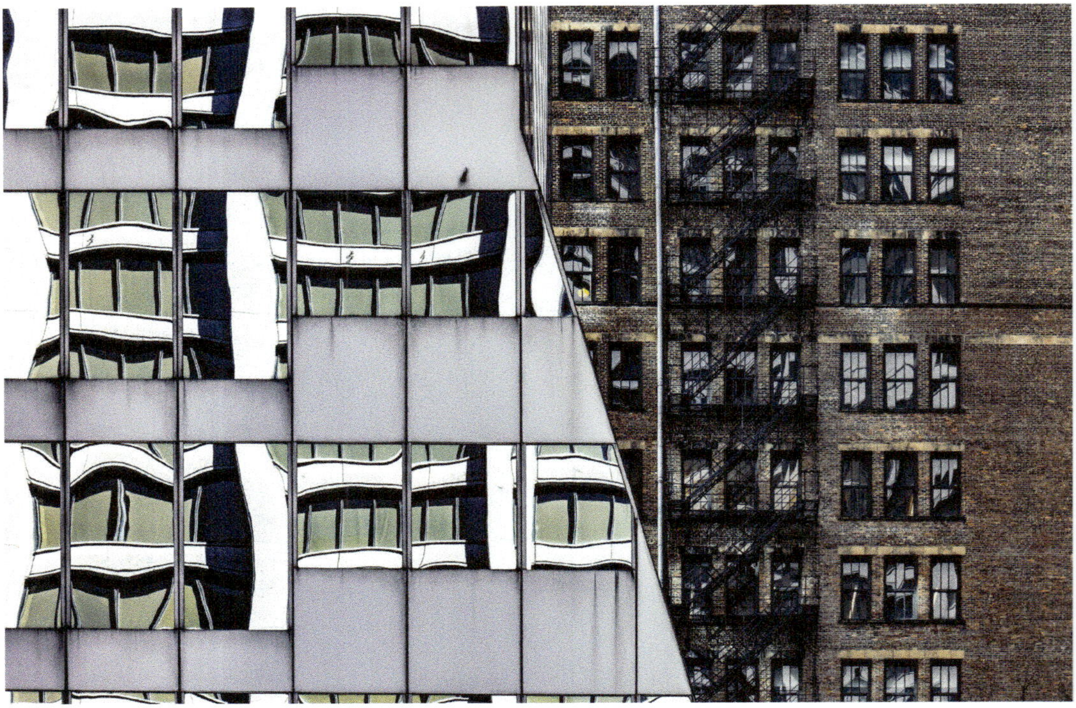

Reflection at 55 West Monroe Street. March 2024.

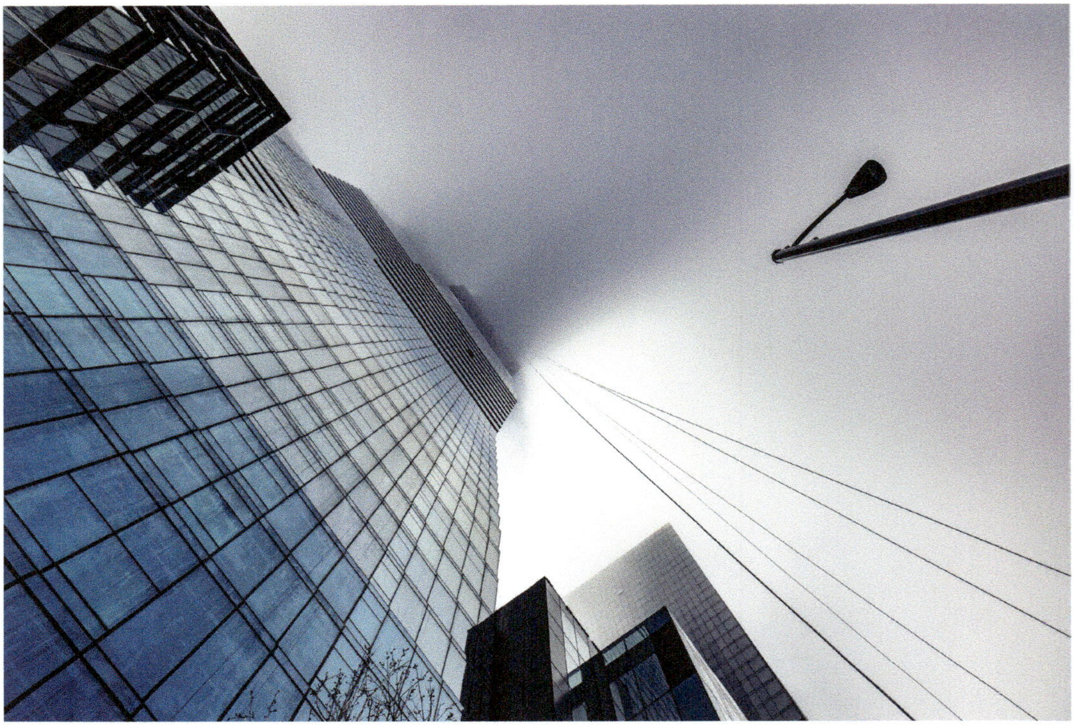

The St. Regis, a new residential skyscraper in Lakeshore East, poking into the clouds. April 2022.

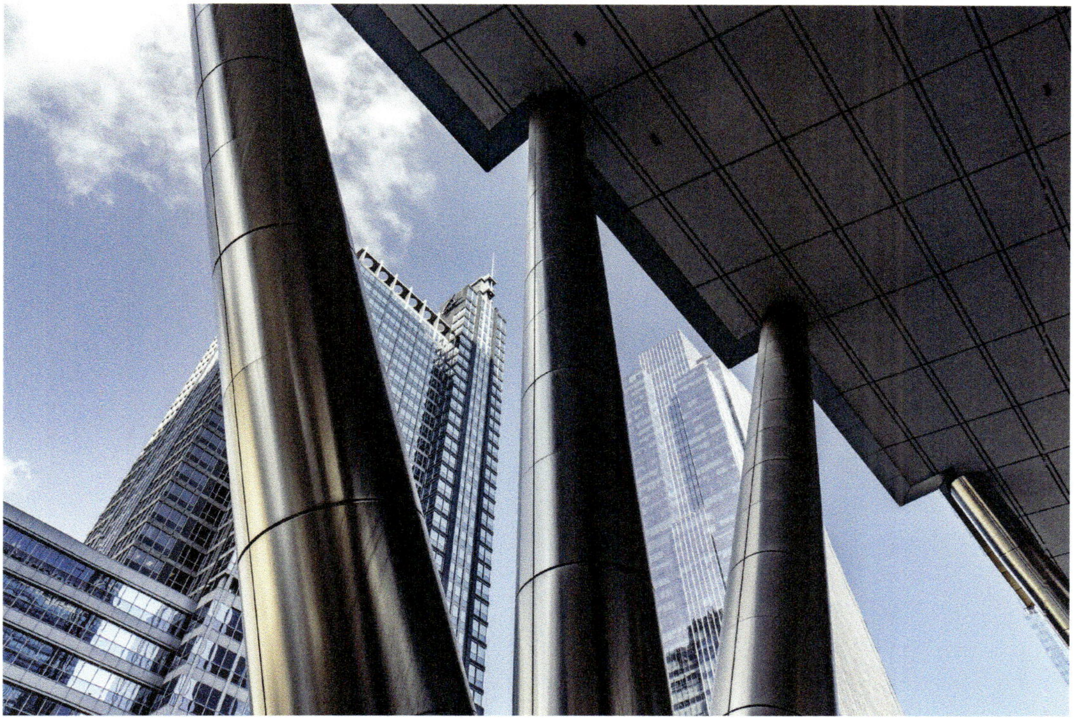

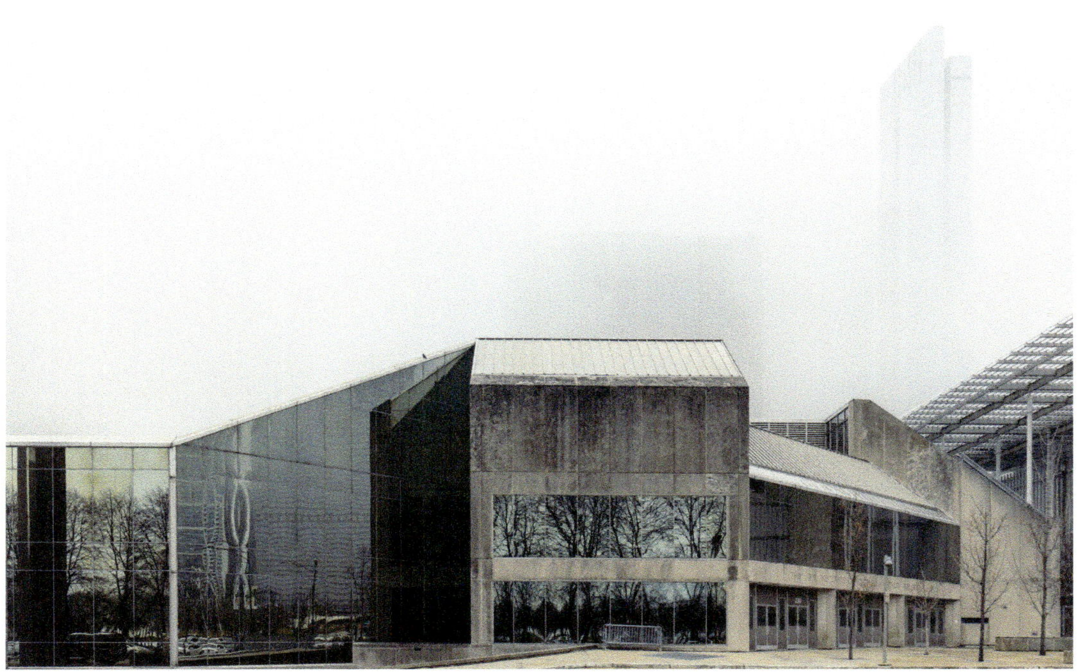

View from the Bank of America Tower. May 2025.

East face of the Art Institute viewed from Columbus Drive. December 2023.

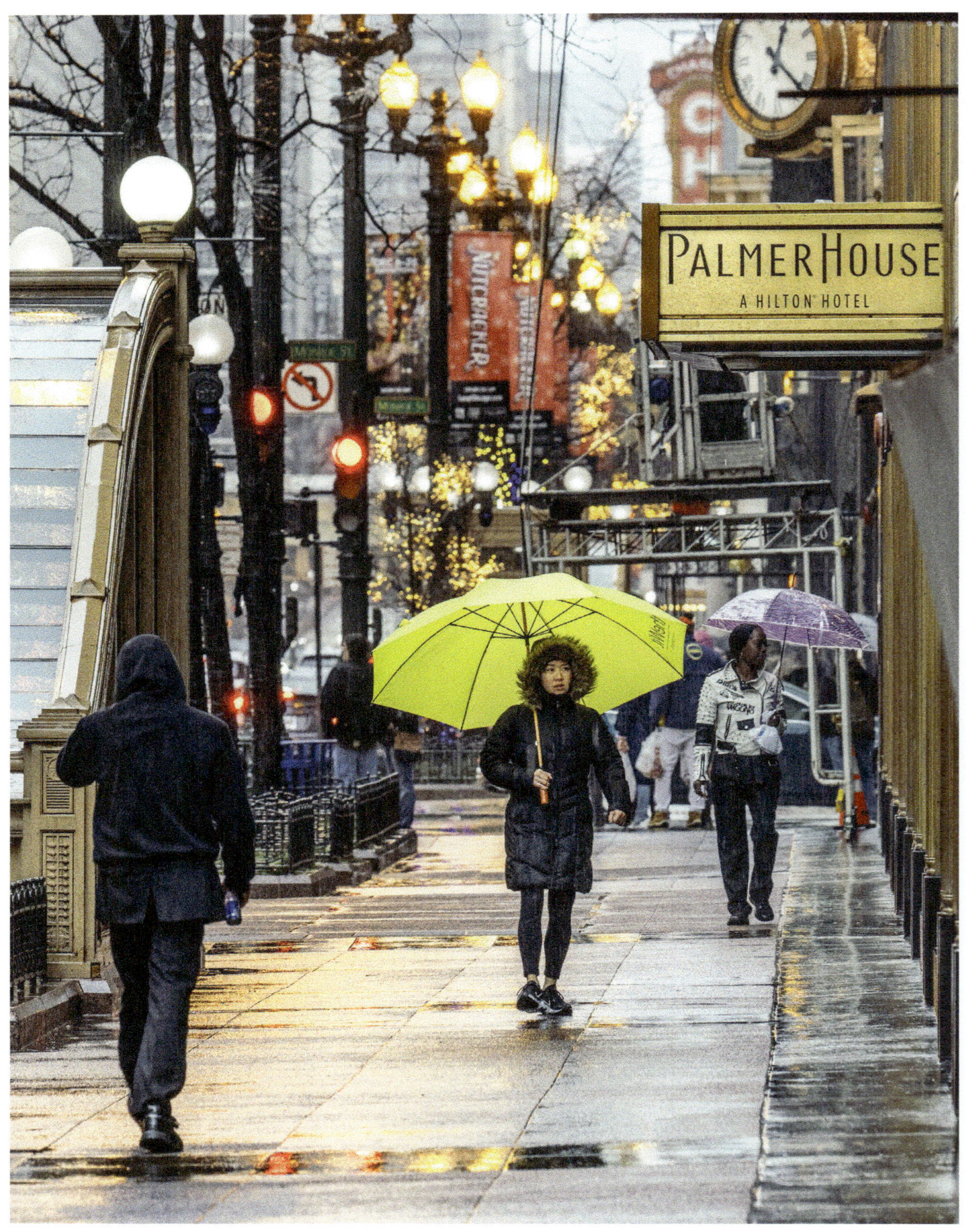

State Street. December 2024.

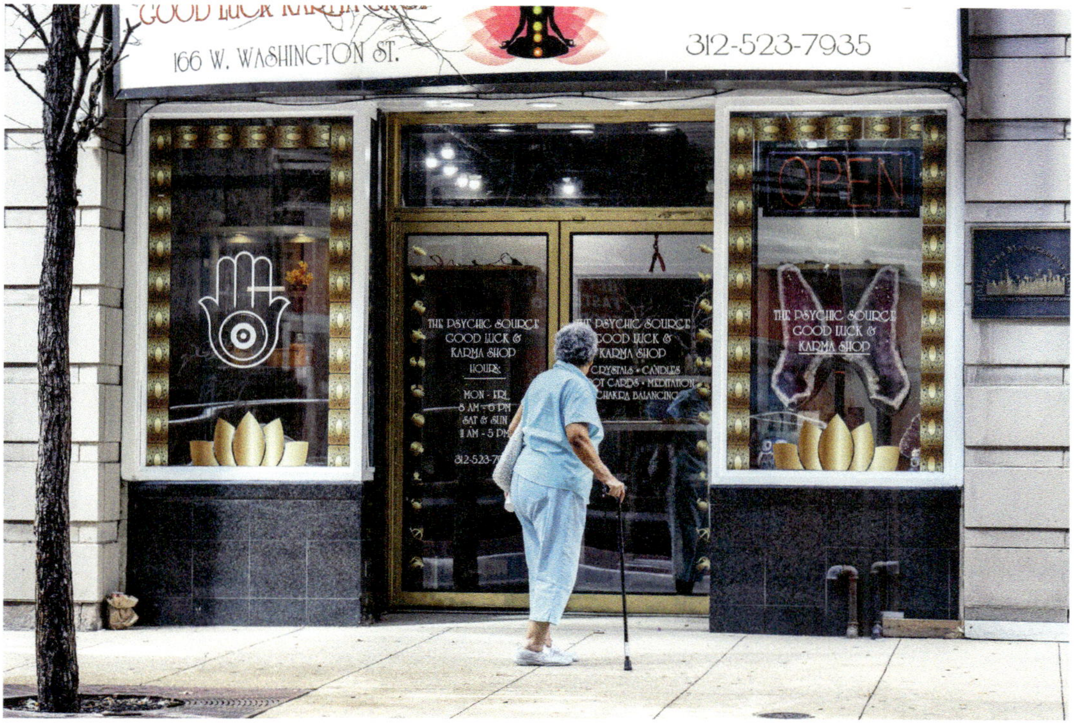

Psychic shop on West Washington Street. August 2022.

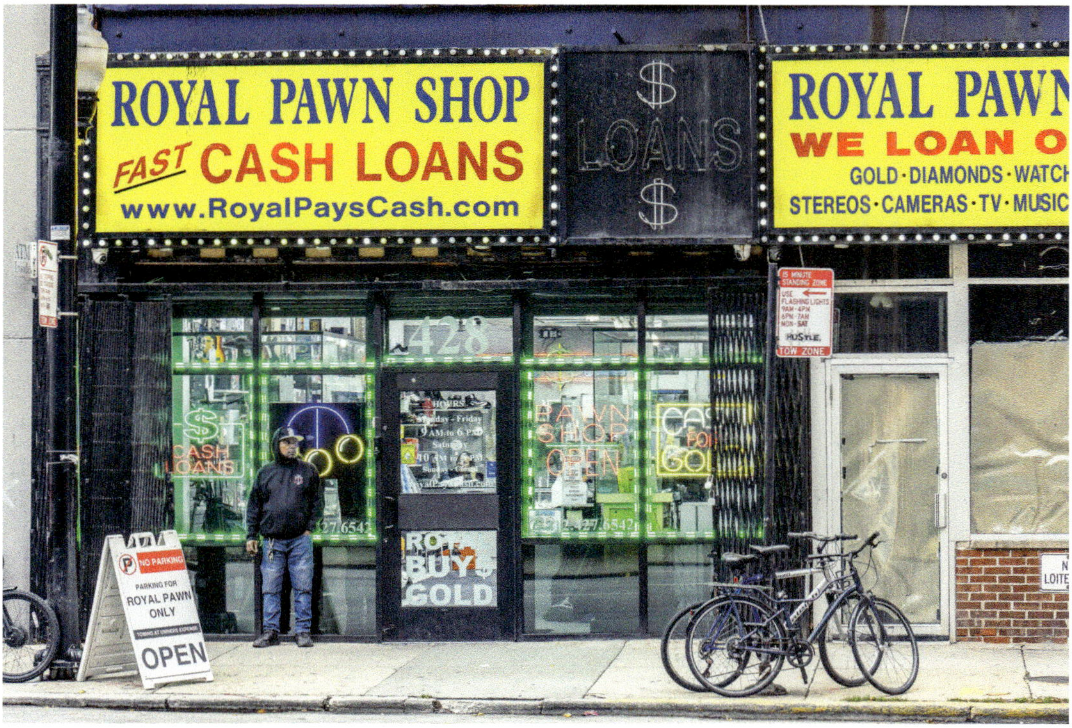

Royal Pawn Shop on South Clark Street. November 2024.

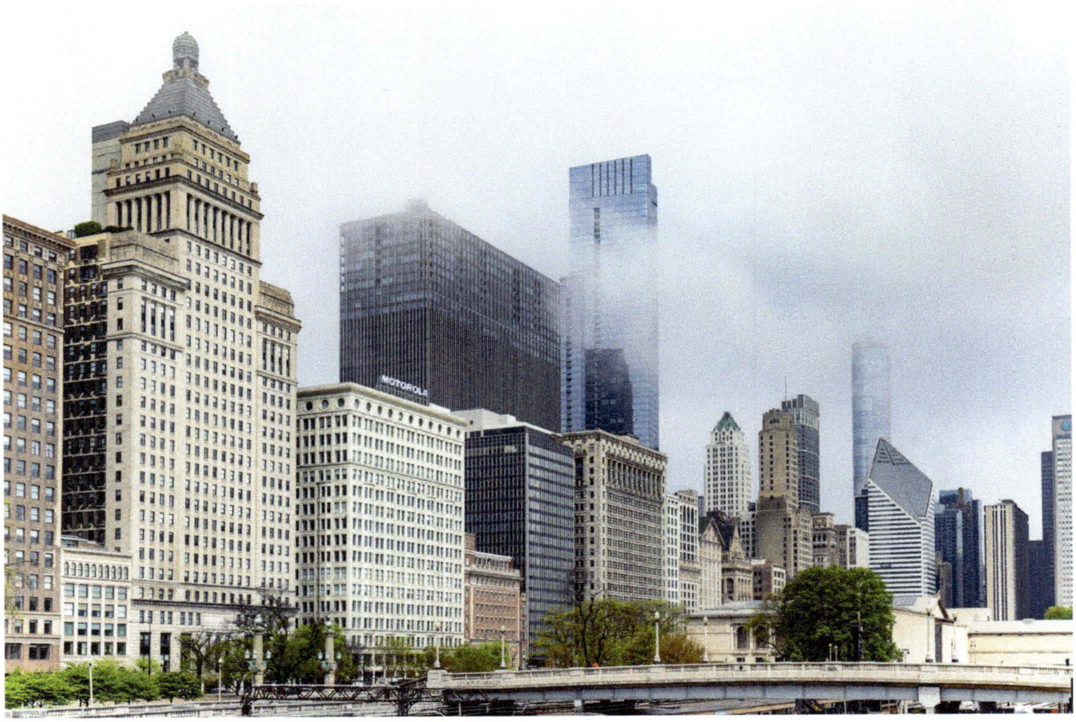

South Michigan Avenue. May 2025.

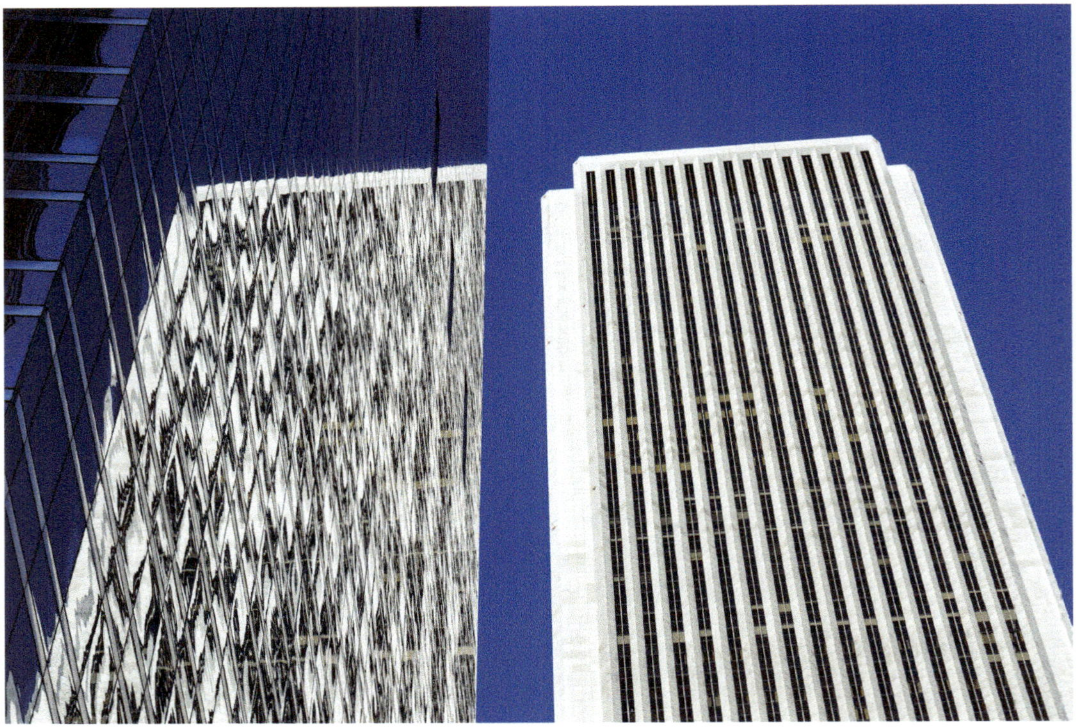

The Aon Center and its reflection in the Blue Cross Blue Shield Tower. April 2014.

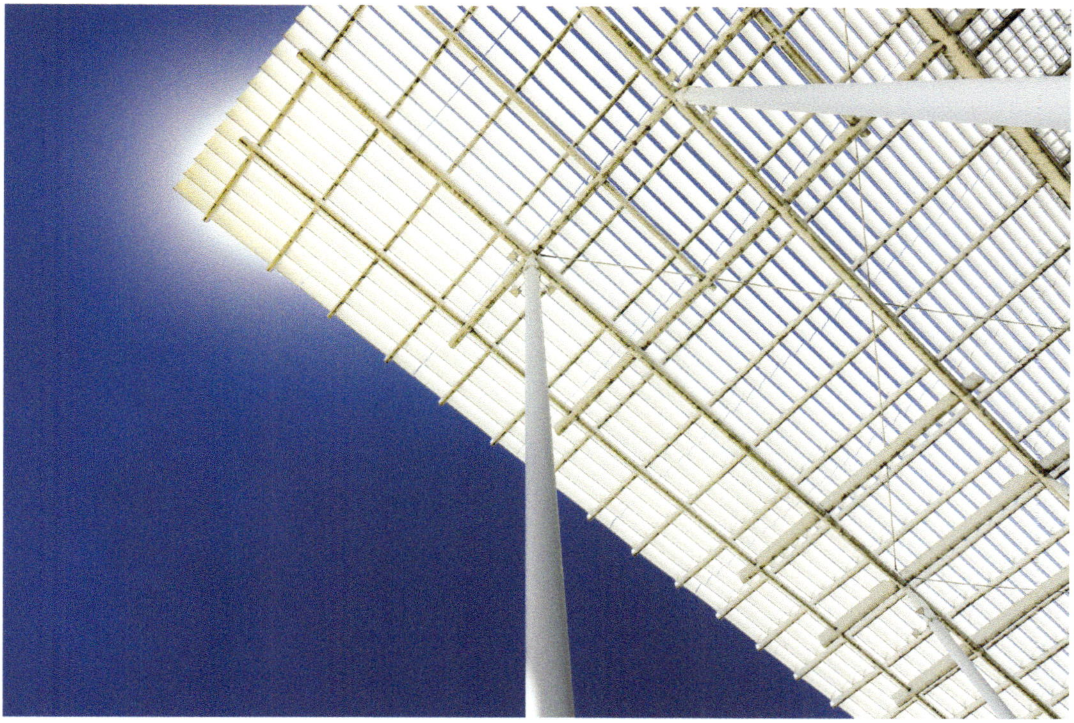

Roof of the Modern Wing of the Art Institute. June 2022.

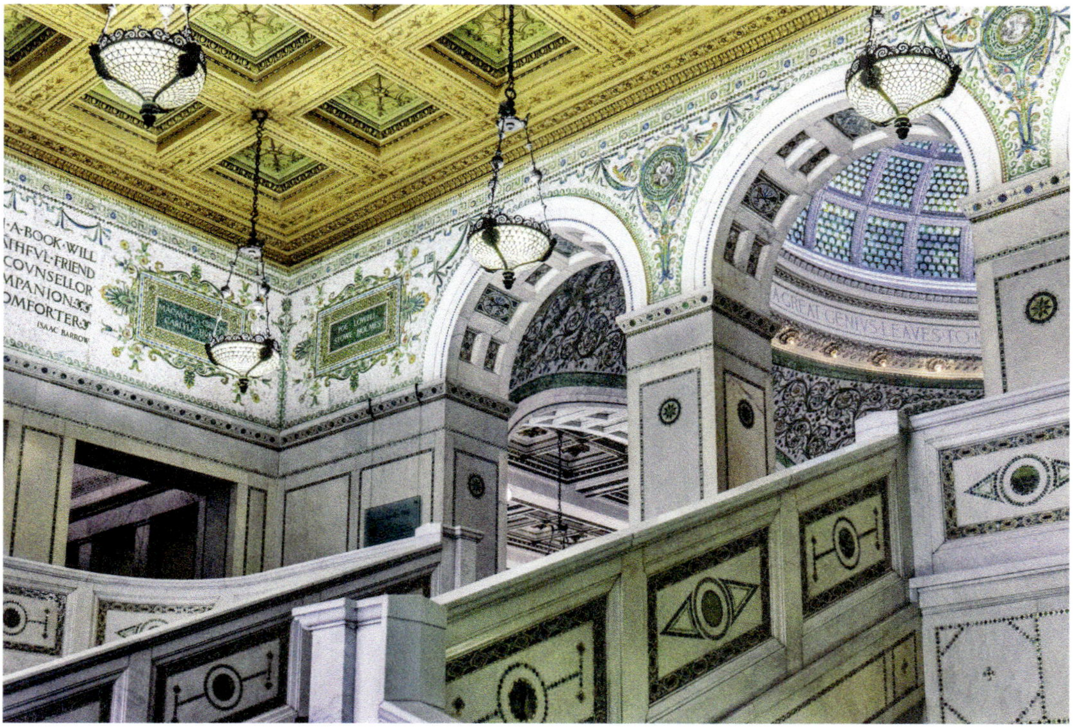

Foyer of the Chicago Cultural Center on Michigan Avenue. December 2015.

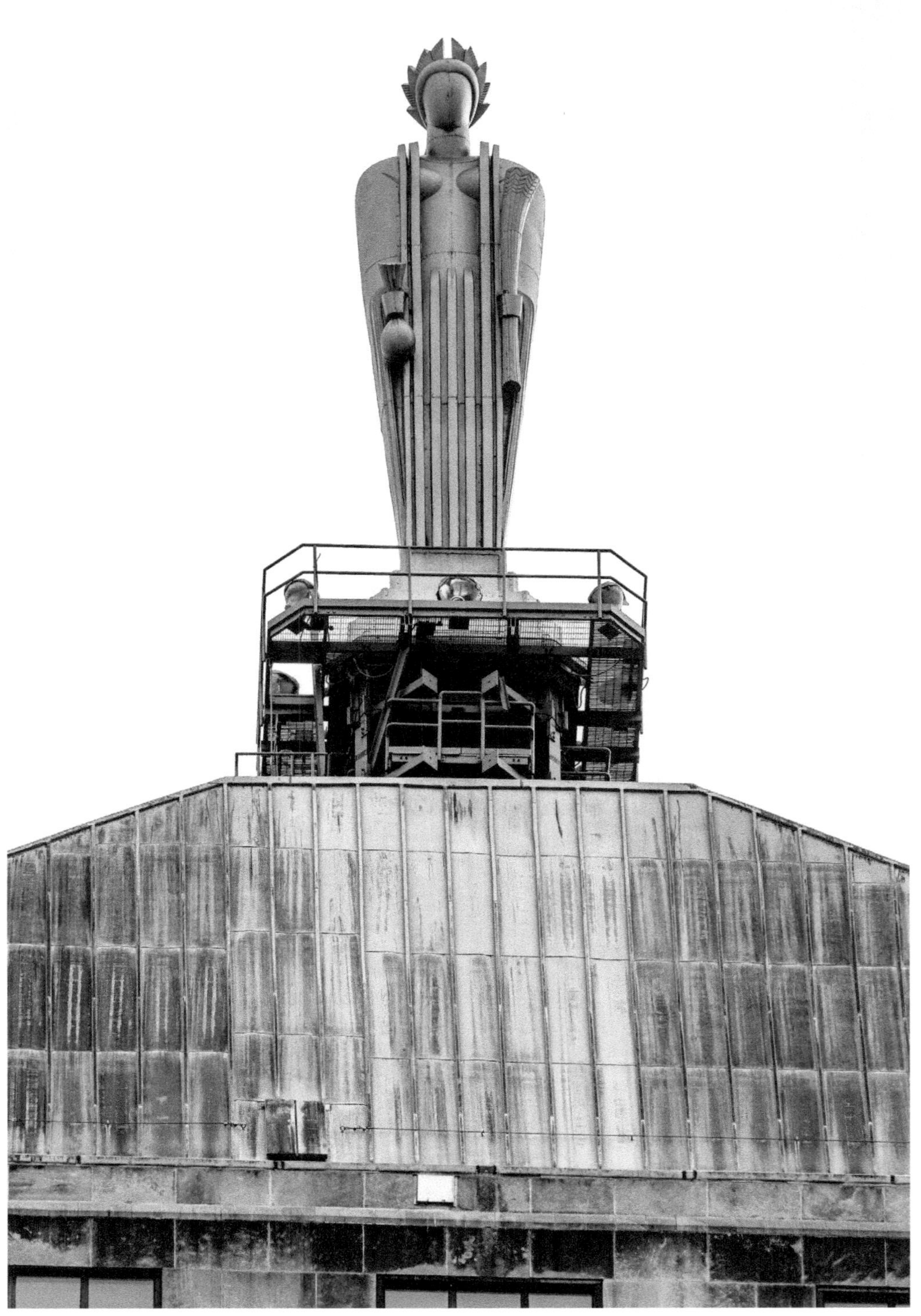

Statue of Ceres on the top of the Chicago Board of Trade at the end of LaSalle Street. March 2024.

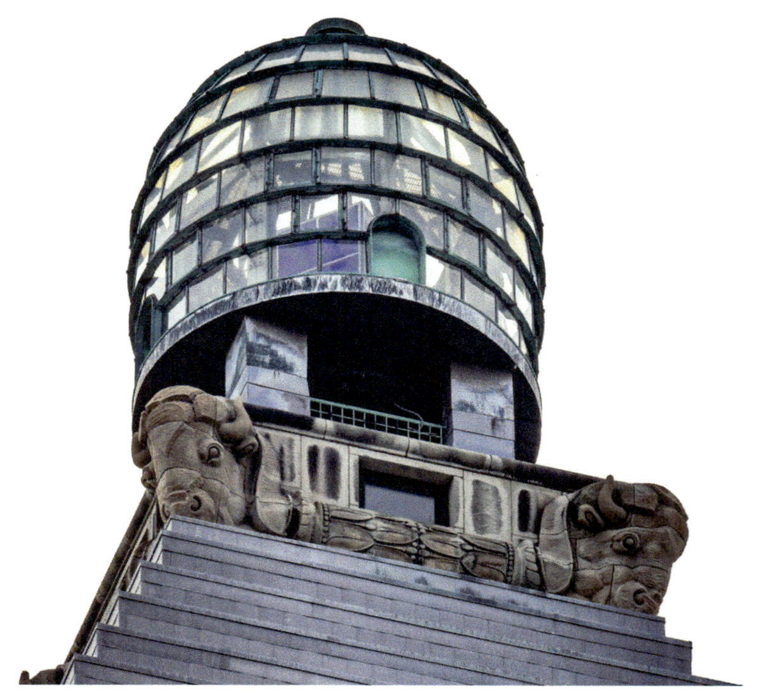

Lantern on the top of The Metropolitan Tower on Michigan Avenue. February 2024.

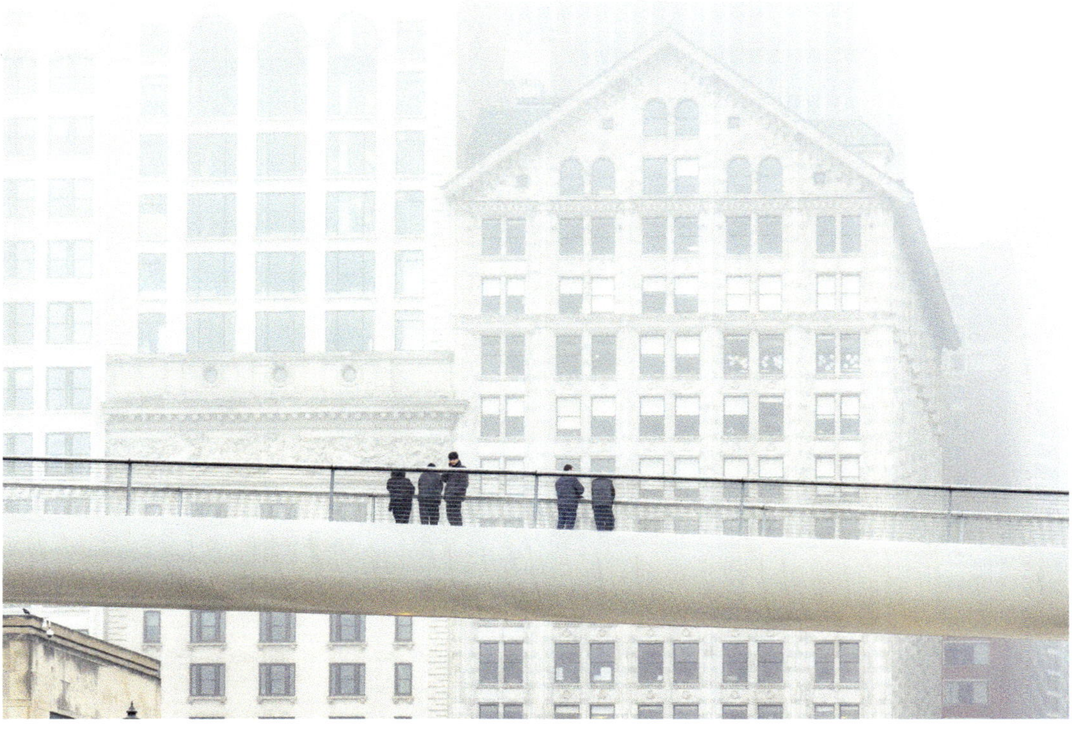

The Nichols Bridgeway across Monroe Street with Michigan Avenue in the background. December 2023.

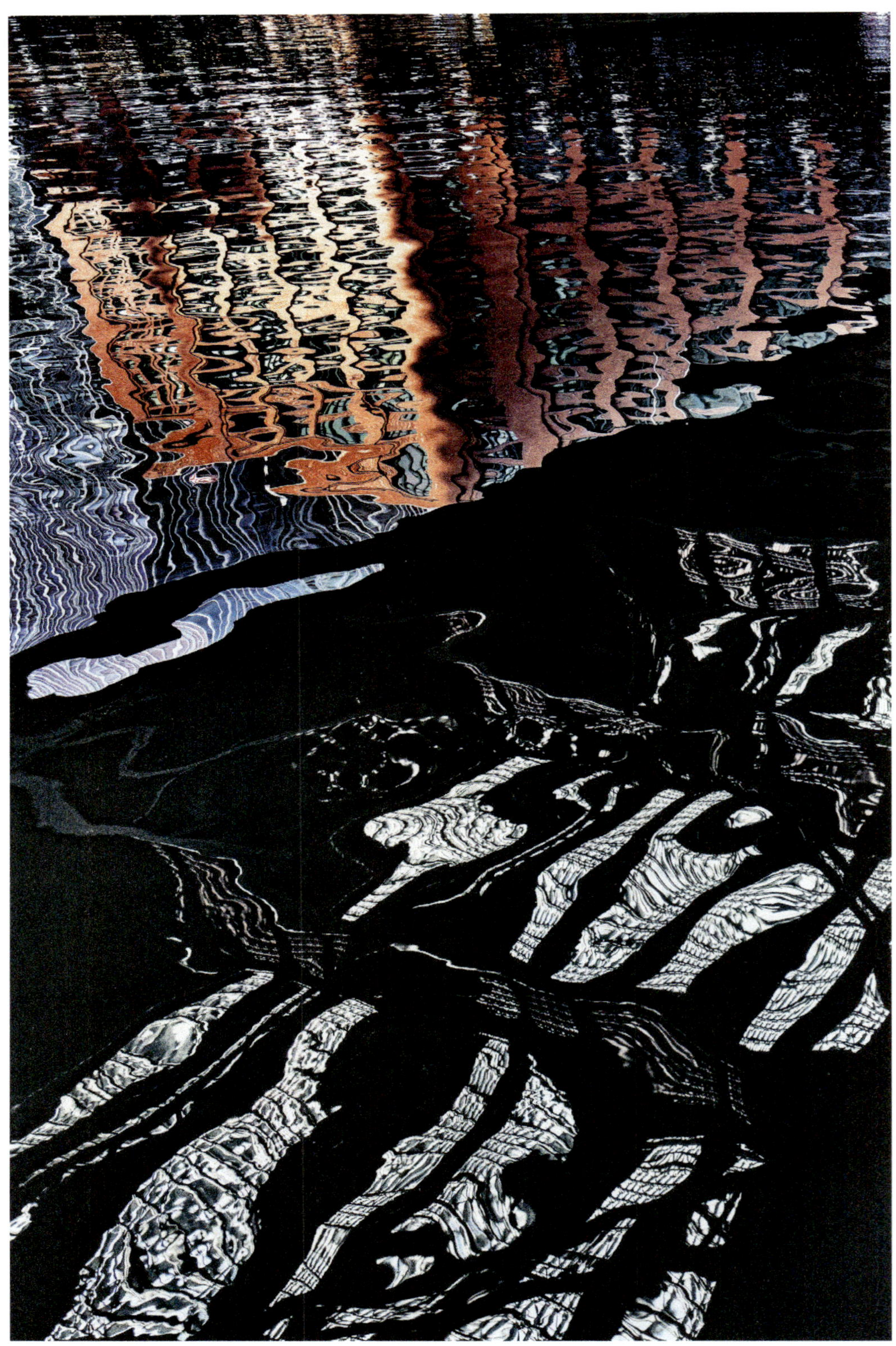

Reflections under Clark Street Bridge. March 2022.

2
The River

The present-day "Main Stem" of the Chicago River flows from Lake Michigan westwards for 1.6 miles to Wolf Point where it splits into the "South Branch" and the "North Branch". Seen from above, the three branches of the river form a "Y." This is the symbol of Chicago displayed on many monuments, lampposts, and other infrastructure within the city. The modern Chicago River has the same general configuration it had in pre-settlement times, but just about everything else has been changed, including where the river meets the lake and the direction of its flow! The latter engineering feat was accomplished in 1900 by deepening the channel so that water flows from Lake Michigan and digging the 28-mile-long Chicago Sanitary and Ship Canal to take the water to the other side of the nearby continental divide (the side that drains away from Lake Michigan and towards the Mississippi).

In the formative days of Chicago, the river was primarily a working harbor and highway. With increasing land values, the docks and warehouses that lined the Main Stem eventually moved away. In recent decades, starting in the 1980s, the Main Stem has been transformed into a river of leisure lined with iconic skyscrapers. At river-level, there is a popular walk along its southern bank. Numerous riverboat tours have knowledgeable guides that point out the main landmarks and describe their history and significance. The tour boats go to the mouth of the river, but most do not enter the lake which is separated from the Main Stem by the Chicago Harbor Lock, built to control the amount of water the river takes from Lake Michigan. There is a good view of the lock from the pedestrian path on the east side of the Lake Shore Drive Bridge.

Chicago is a city of river bridges. There are twenty of them that cross the river from the Loop. They open at scheduled times between April and November to allow the passage of tall-masted yachts. The bridges have bridge-houses which are the control centers for the openings. The one at the southwest corner of the Michigan Avenue Bridge is also a museum. You can enter from the river level and see the bridge-raising machinery. You can also see an obsolete bridge-raising mechanism under the Chicago Avenue Bridge from the North Branch riverwalk on the east bank.

There are some special times when the river becomes a visual spectacle. The Main Stem is dyed bright green on the Saturday of the Saint Patrick's Day parade in March. The eco-friendly green dye is applied to the river by members of the Chicago Journeyman Plumbers Union. The dye, which is normally used to detect leaks in buildings, starts off bright orange and then, by some secret plumber's magic, turns iridescent green in the water. It is a sight to behold. The river bridges over the colorful river are packed shoulder-to-shoulder with people enjoying the plumber's performance. The second special river spectacle also occurs in winter. After the water has lost its summer heat, the river can freeze. Not the whole river, just the top layer which becomes decorated with broken ice. This cold finger pokes into the heart of the city from Lake Michigan, sometimes as far as Wolf Point. Sunlight and city lights are reflected from the ice and, when it's newly washed and wet by a passing icebreaker, the frozen water also reflects the cityscape. Skyscrapers are transformed into two-dimensional geometric forms with occasional splashes of glowing reds, greens, and yellows captured within the blue-tinted ice floes. This magical phenomenon usually happens on the coldest days in January and February.

In the summer the Main Stem is a busy thoroughfare with tour boats, water taxis, kayaks, and occasionally a bright red fireboat or a floating hot tub! The bridges provide good bird's-eye views of this water traffic. There are also plenty of places along the riverwalk to sit and watch the passing boats. For some extra excitement, on the north bank of the river, roughly half-way between the Columbus Drive Bridge and Lake Shore Drive Bridge, there is a water canon that shoots an 80-foot water arc across the river every hour, on the hour between 8 a.m. and 11 p.m. Tour boats time their passage to either keep their passengers dry, or perhaps get them a little wet. The water canon is part of the Centennial Fountain, dedicated in 1989 to celebrate the 100th anniversary of the Metropolitan Water Reclamation District of Greater Chicago, the entity that was responsible for reversing the flow of the river.

Photographer Tips

i) After being dyed for St. Patrick's Day celebrations, the river stays green for a day or two. The day after dyeing is a good time to see the river without the crowds.

ii) The appearance of the frozen river changes with the time of day and cloud cover. For abstract photographs, it's worth revisiting several times.

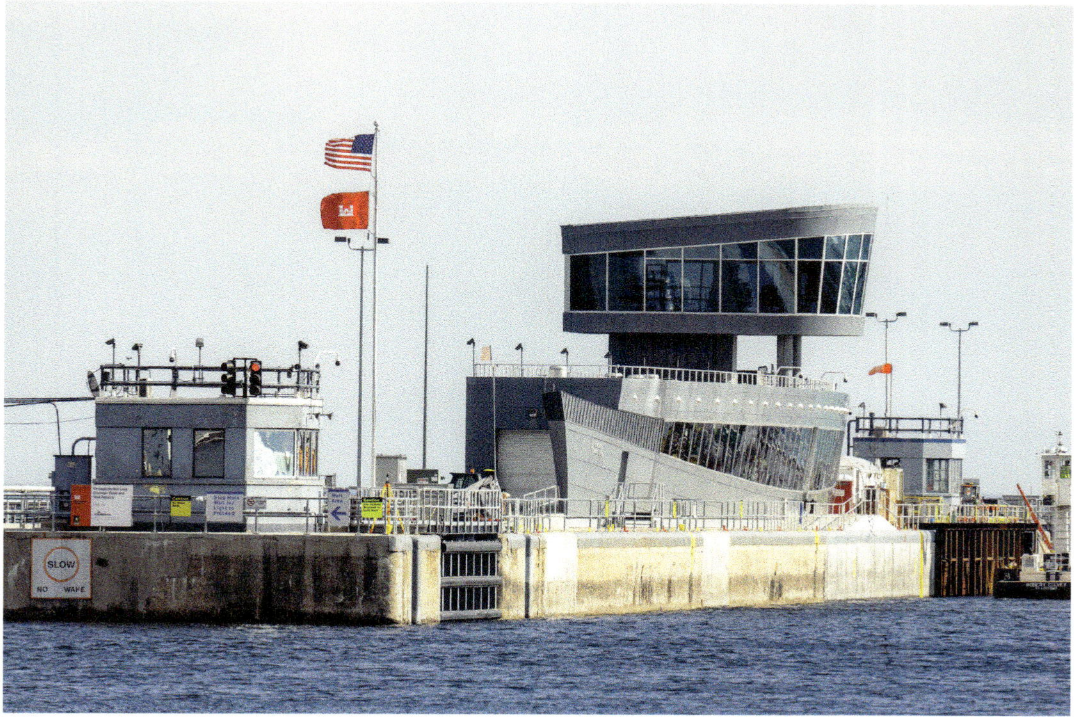

The Chicago Harbor Lock, also known as the Chicago River and Harbor Controlling Works. February 2024.

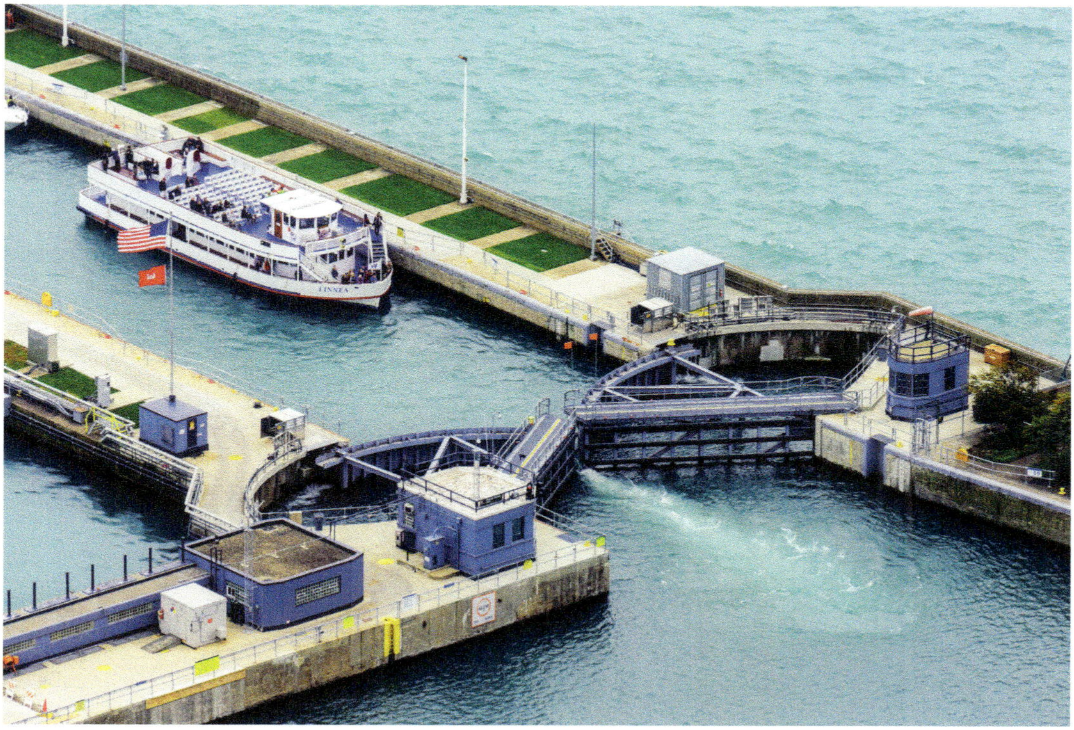

The Chicago Harbor Lock. October 2016.

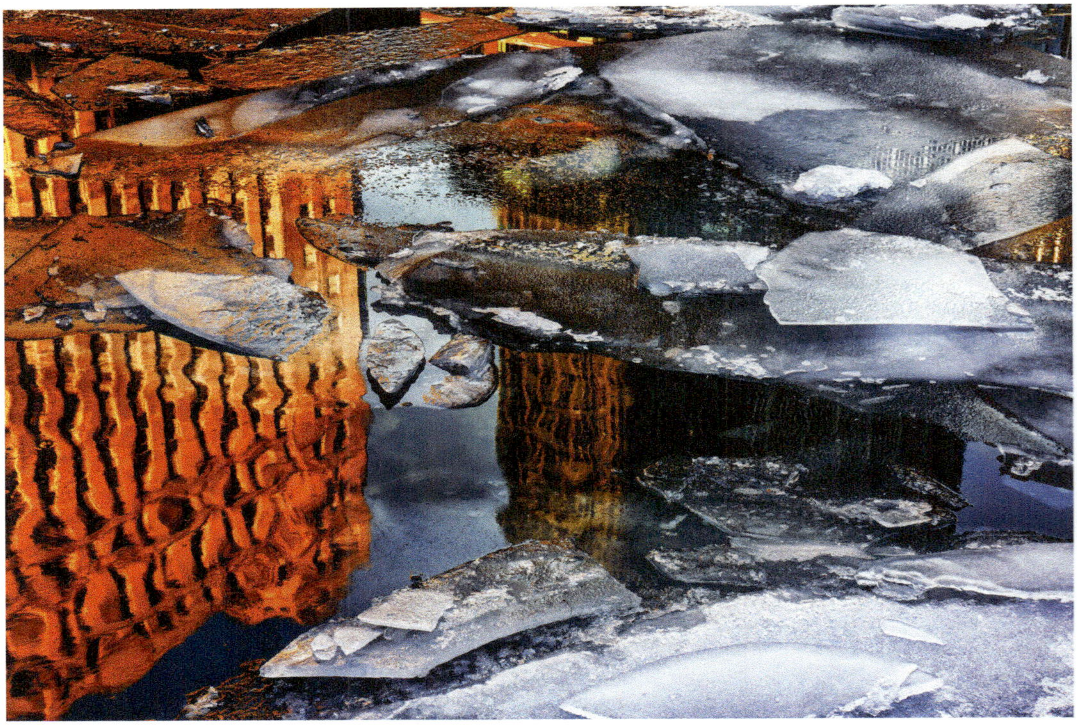

Frozen Chicago River at sunset. January 2018.

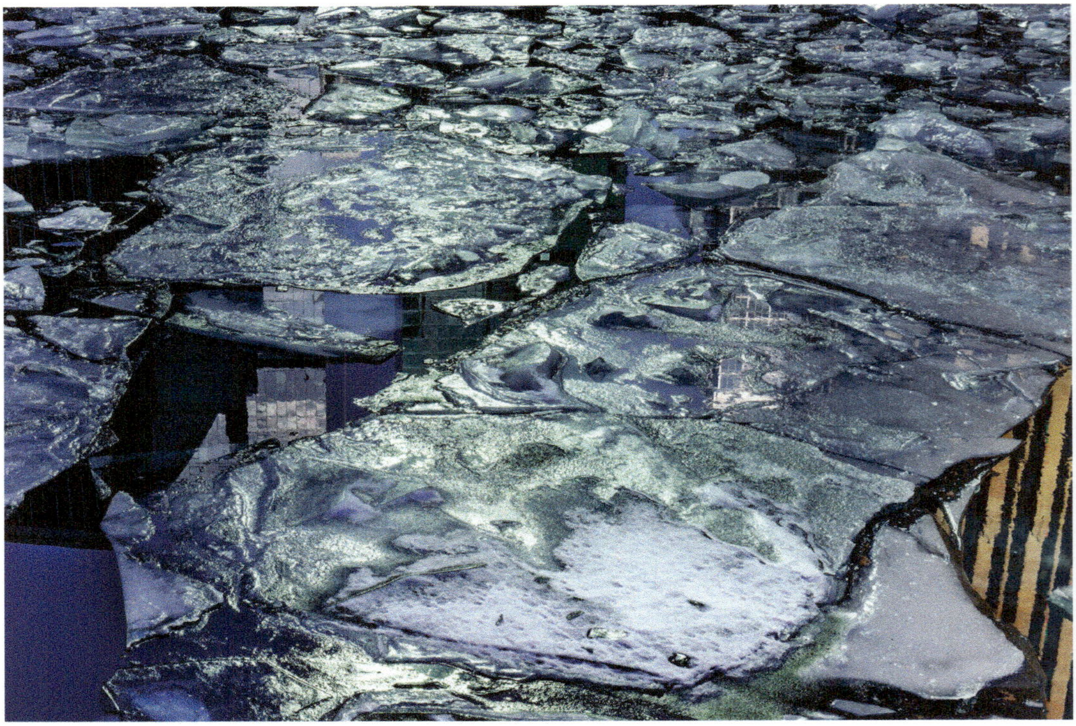

Frozen Chicago River. January 2018.

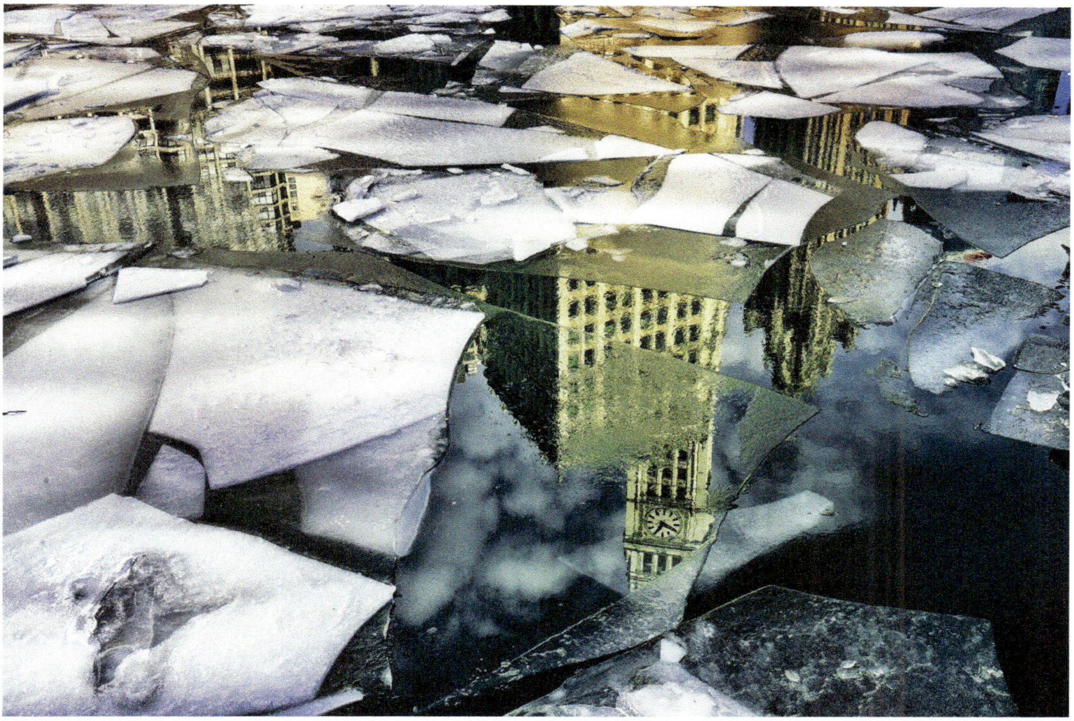

Wrigley Building Clock Tower reflected in the frozen Chicago River. January 2018.

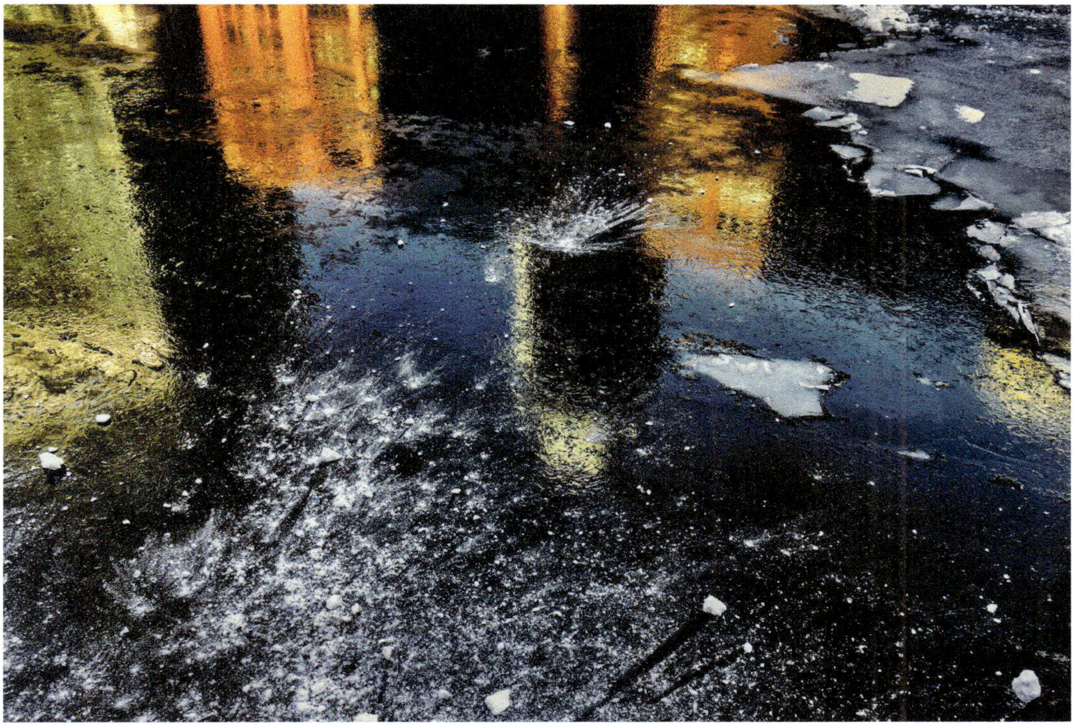

Frozen Chicago River. January 2022.

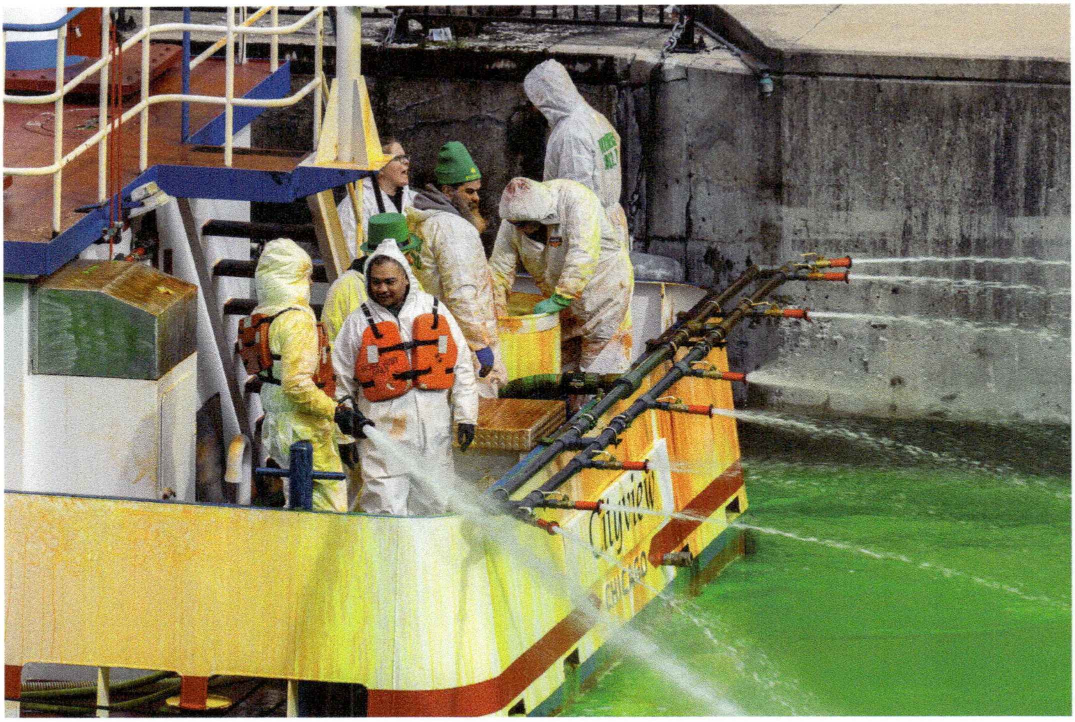

Dyeing the Chicago River green, St. Patrick's Day weekend. March 2024.

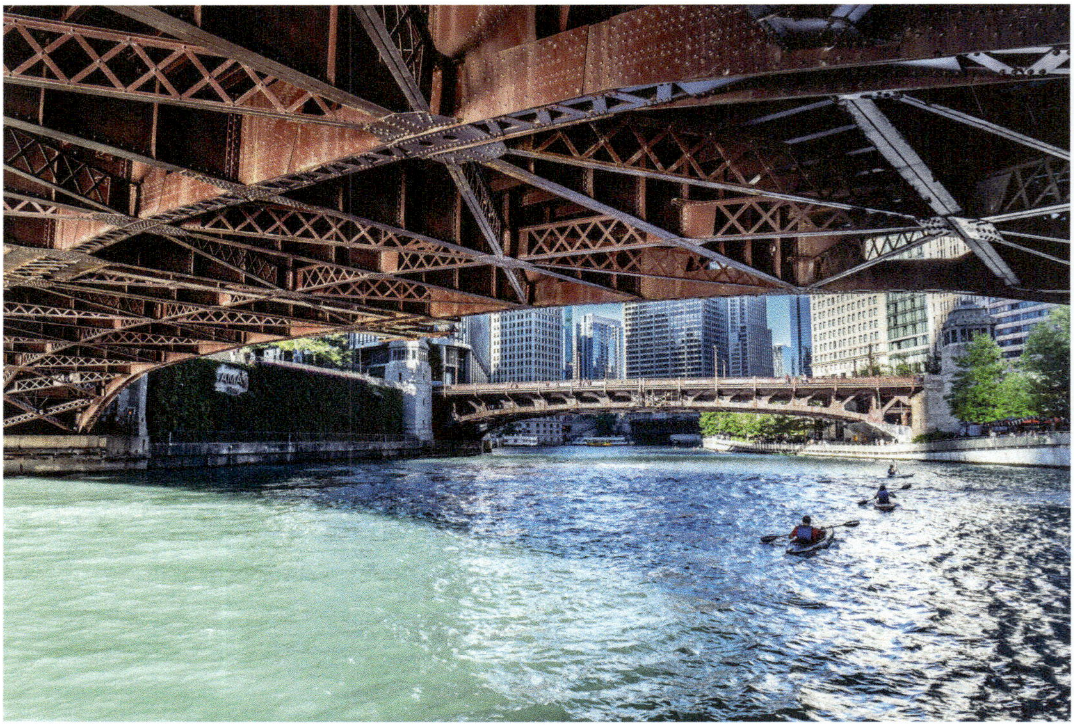

Wabash Avenue Bridge viewed from under State Street Bridge. September 2018.

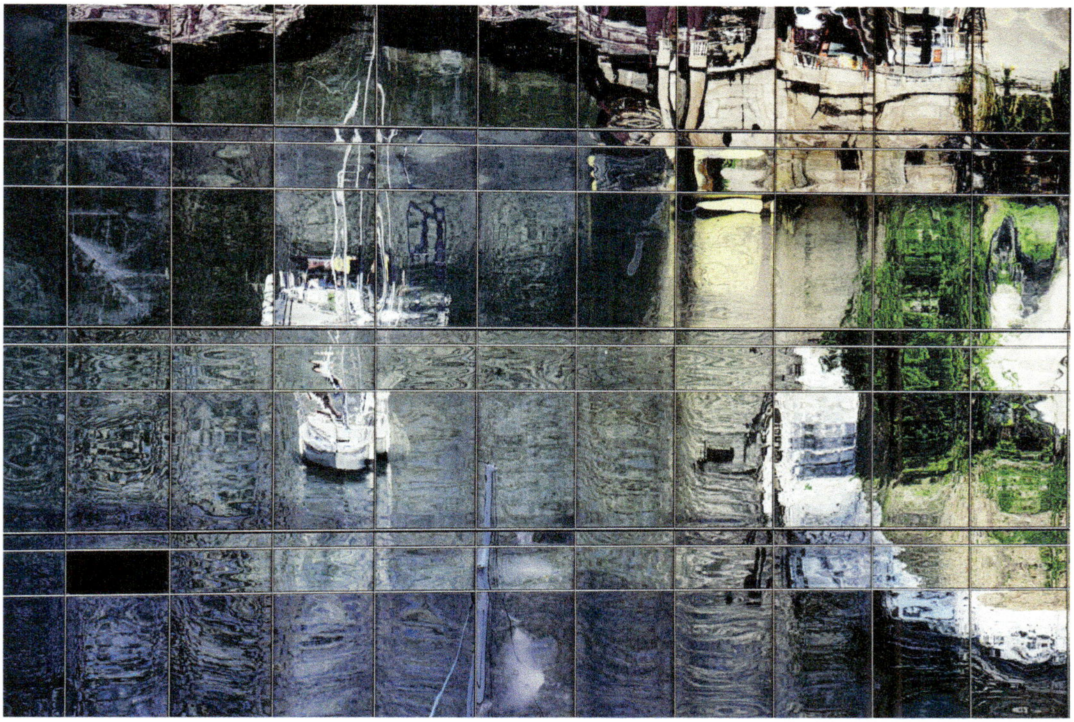

Chicago River at Wolf Point reflected in the windows of the River Point skyscraper. May 2016.

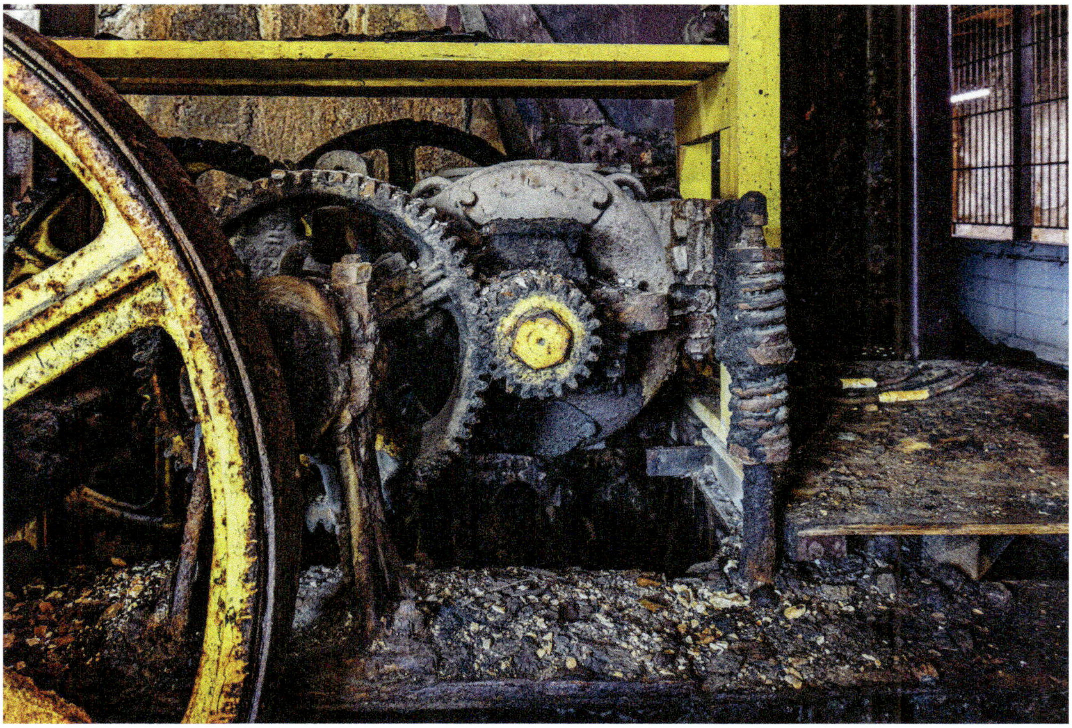

Obsolete bridge raising mechanism. Chicago Avenue Bridge, December 2023.

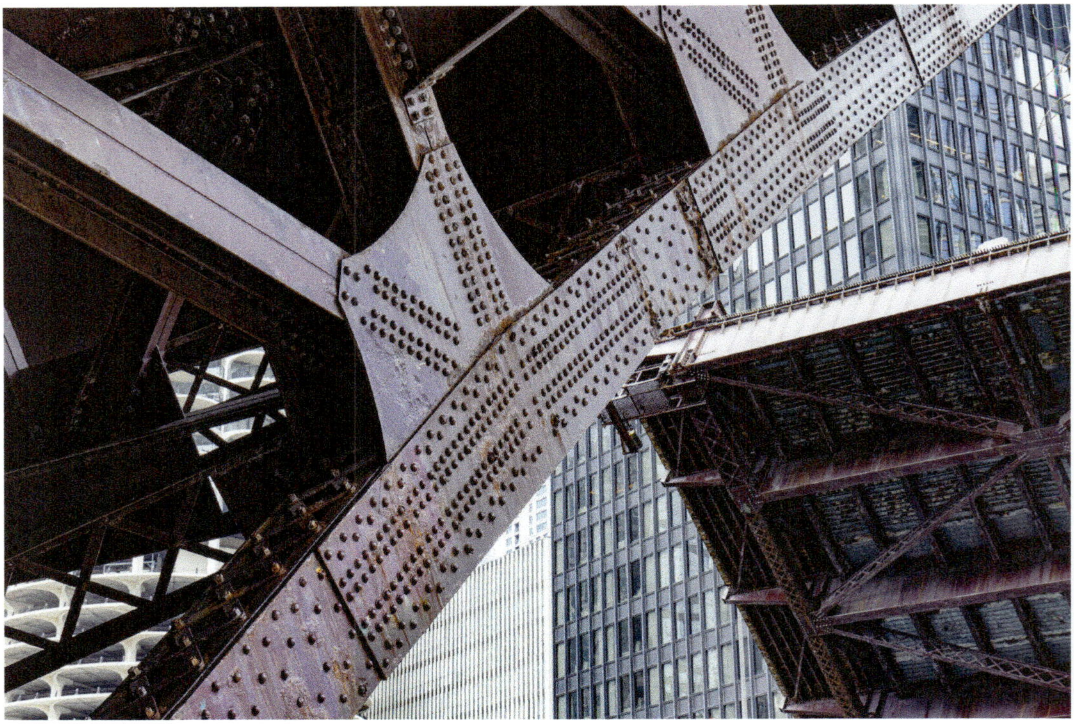

Wabash Avenue Bridge raised. April 2025.

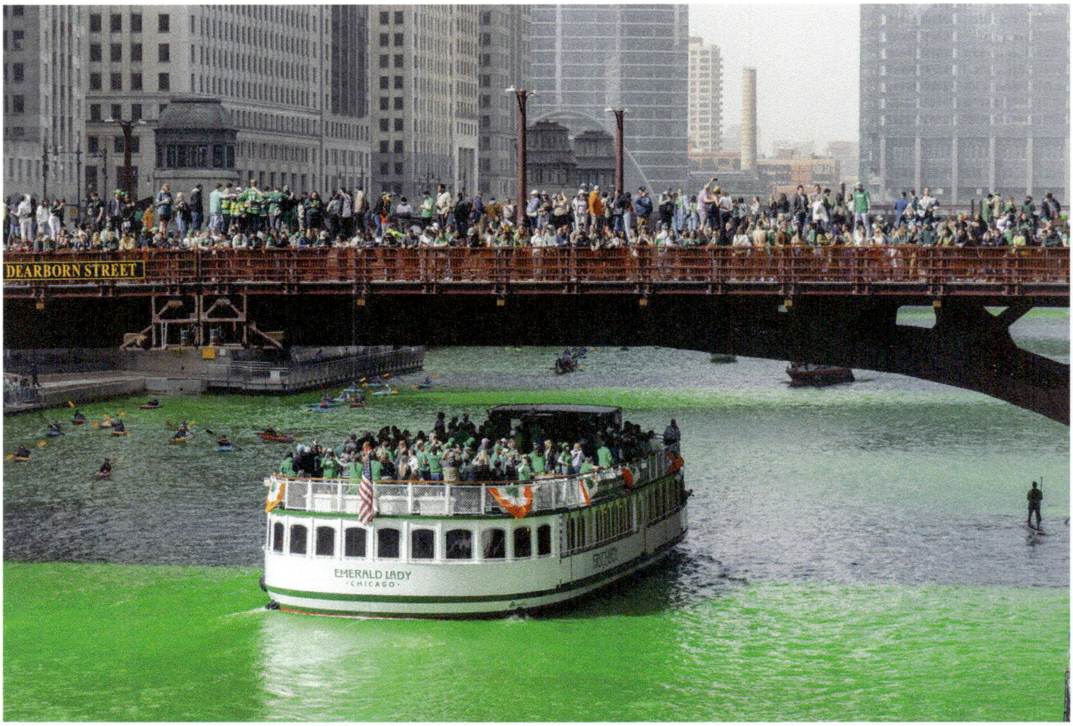

The river dyed green for the St. Patrick's Day celebrations. March 2025.

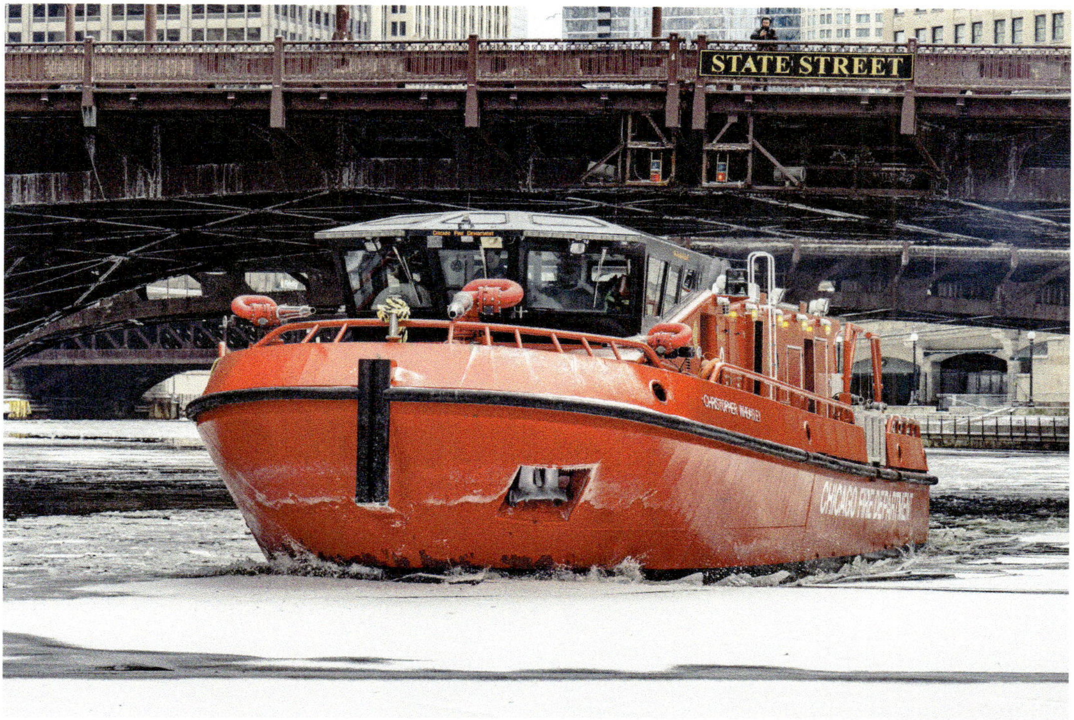

The *Christopher Wheatley*, a Chicago fireboat, breaking ice on the Main Stem of the Chicago River. January 2025.

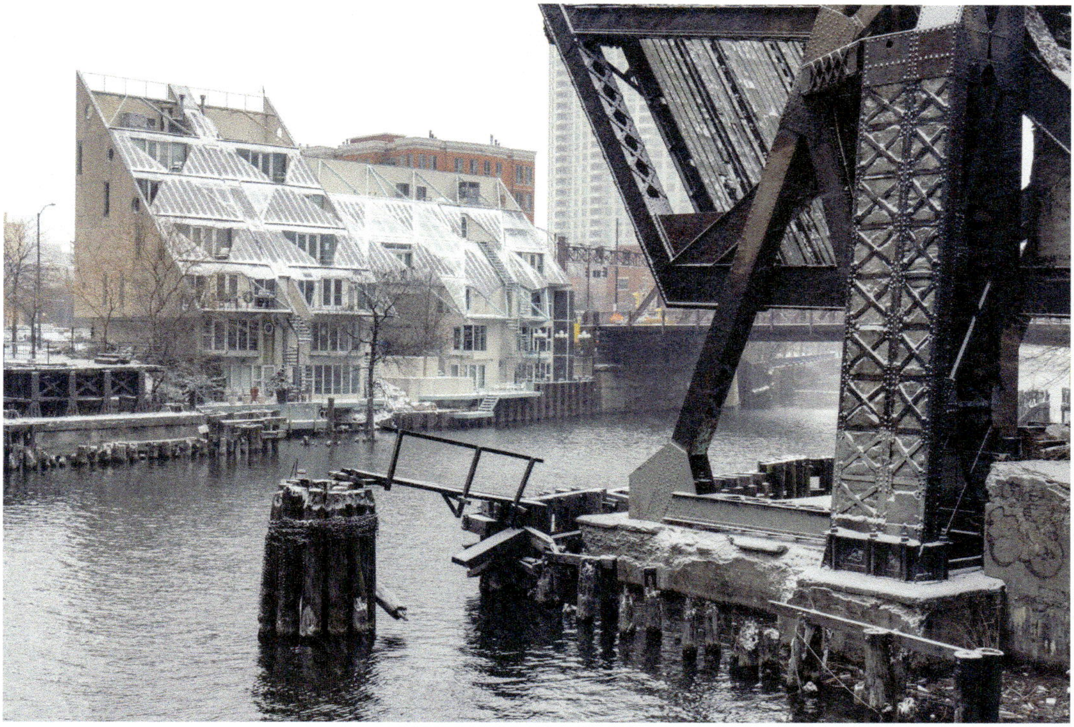

The River Cottages, North Branch of the Chicago River. February 2025.

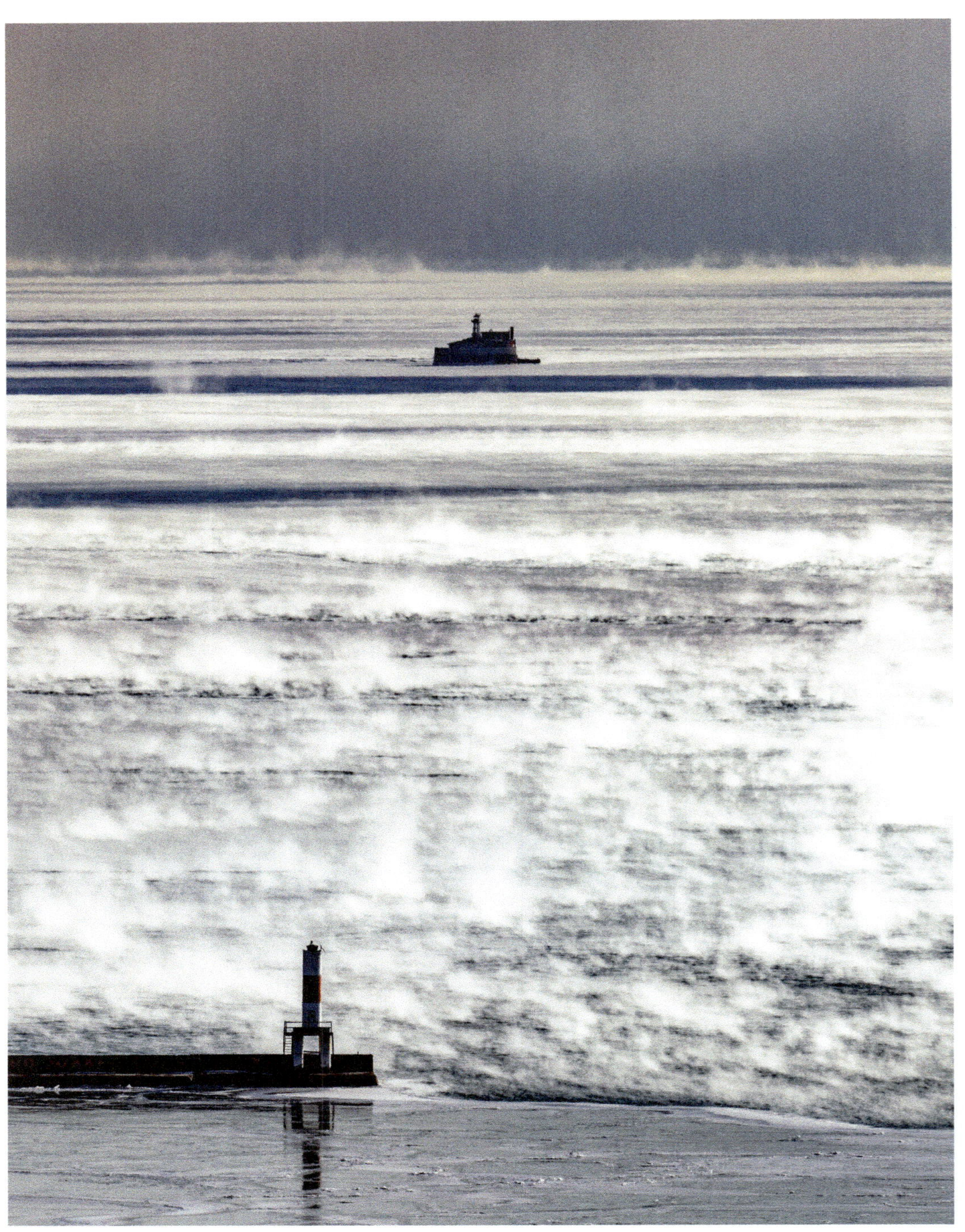

Lake Michigan steaming. The air temperature was -6°F. Water crib in the distance. January 2025.

3
The Lake

Lake Michigan has justifiably been called an inland sea. It exhibits all the moods of an ocean. It can be as calm as a mill pond or wild, stormy, and dangerous. In winter the lake surface sometimes freezes, and on exceptionally cold days, the frigid water can steam.

Chicago's lakefront is almost entirely open to the public. Remarkably, 26 miles out of its 30-mile length are accessible, and for 18.5 miles there is the Lakefront Trail. Along the way there are parks, sandy beaches, harbors, and fishing piers. Two of the most popular beaches are downtown: the Ohio Street Beach and Oak Street Beach. From May until October, pleasure boats fill the harbor docks and at the weekends the lake close to shore is often busy with sailing yachts and motorboats. For the winter months many of these are stored at local boat yards. Offshore, there are breakwaters, lighthouses, and six large cylindrical fort-like structures. These are the water cribs. Located roughly 2 miles offshore, they were built to provide intakes for the city's drinking water. Only two are still active.

The most popular annual lakefront event is the visually spectacular Chicago Air and Water Show. It occurs over an August weekend and is the largest free event of its kind in the United States. The main permanent visitor attraction on the lakefront is Navy Pier which pokes 1 mile into Lake Michigan. On the pier there are many shops and places to eat, the Chicago Shakespeare Theater, a hotel, and a giant Ferris wheel. The end of the pier is the closest you can get on foot to the iconic Harbor Lighthouse.

Photographer Tips

i) In the summer months, for great views of the Loop from the lake you can take a water taxi from Navy Pier to the Museum Campus.

ii) Just north of Navy Pier, Olive Park has nice views of the Streeterville lakefront.

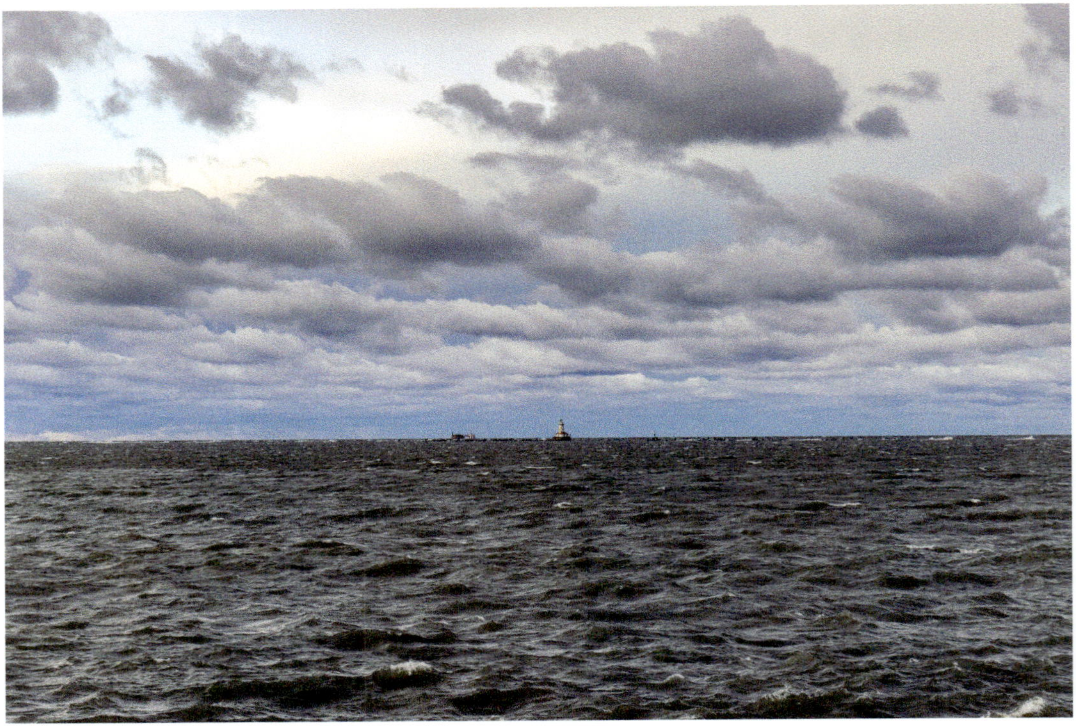

Monroe Harbor. September 2021.

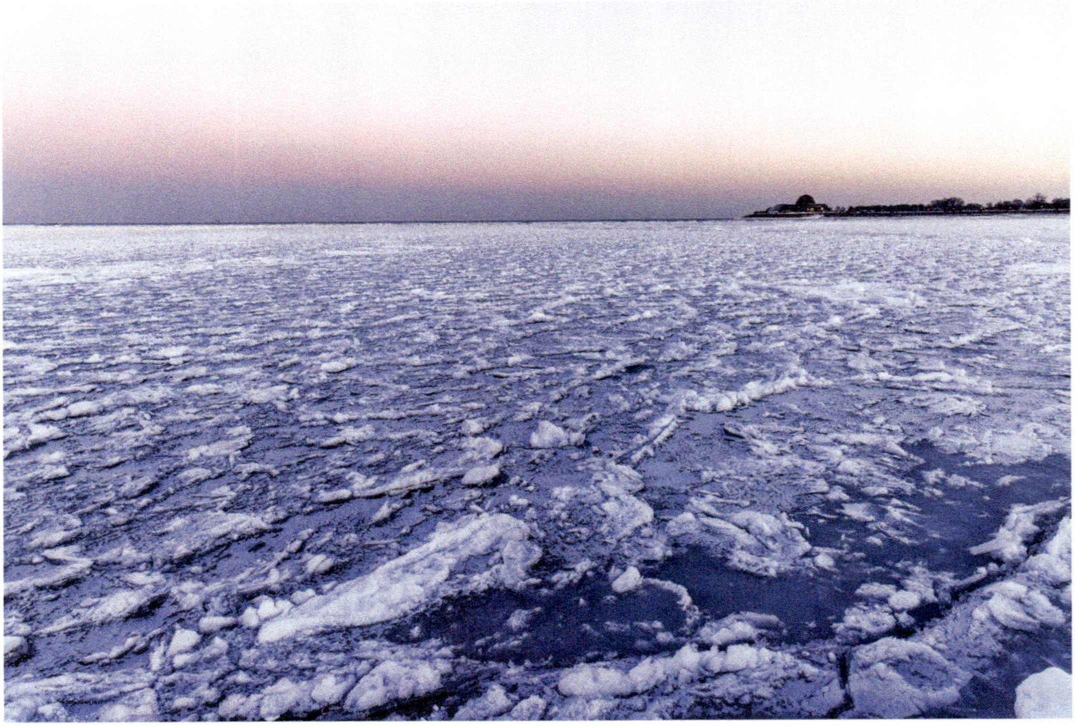

Monroe Harbor. February 2022.

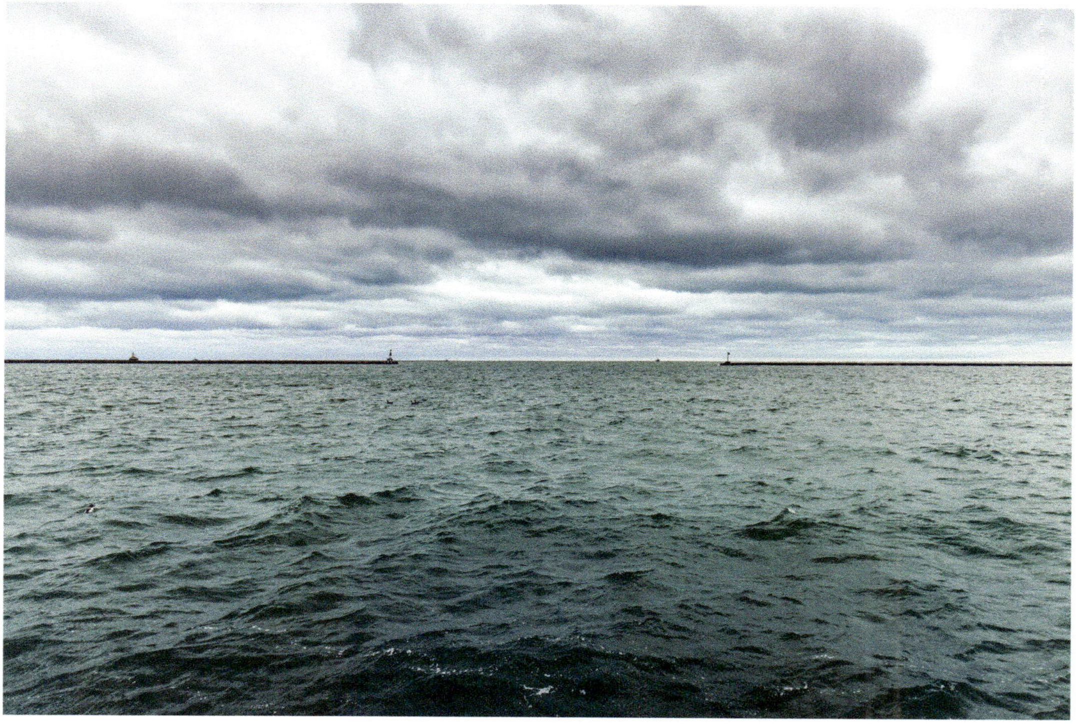

Monroe Harbor. February 2025.

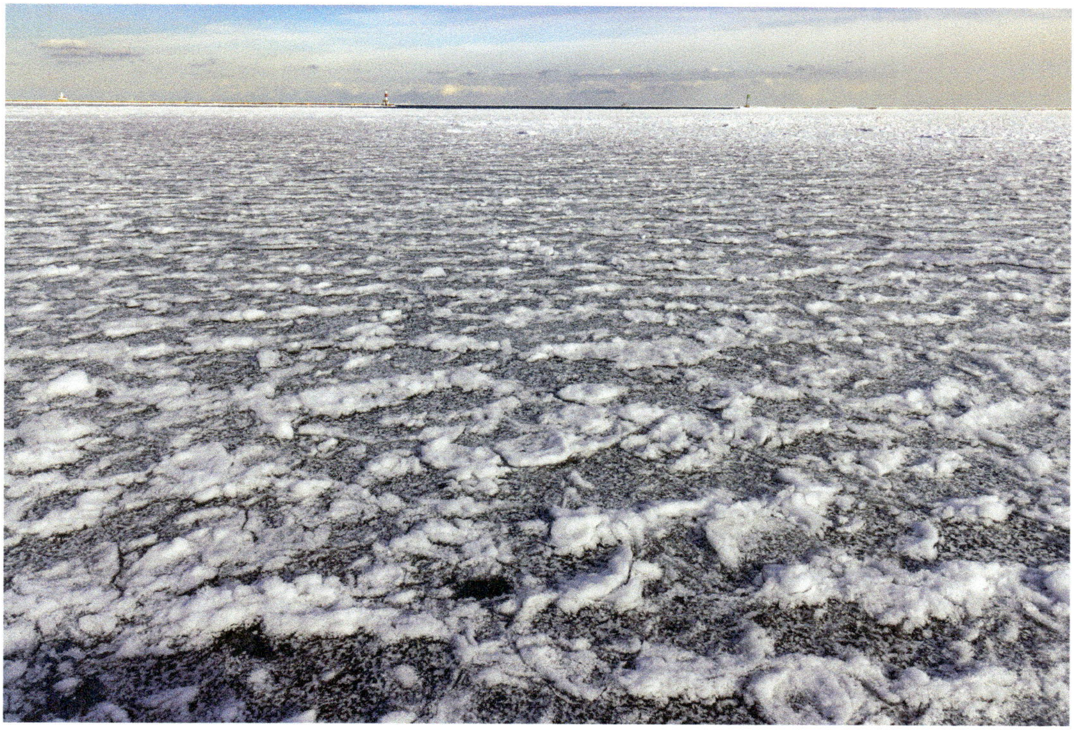

Monroe Harbor. February 2022.

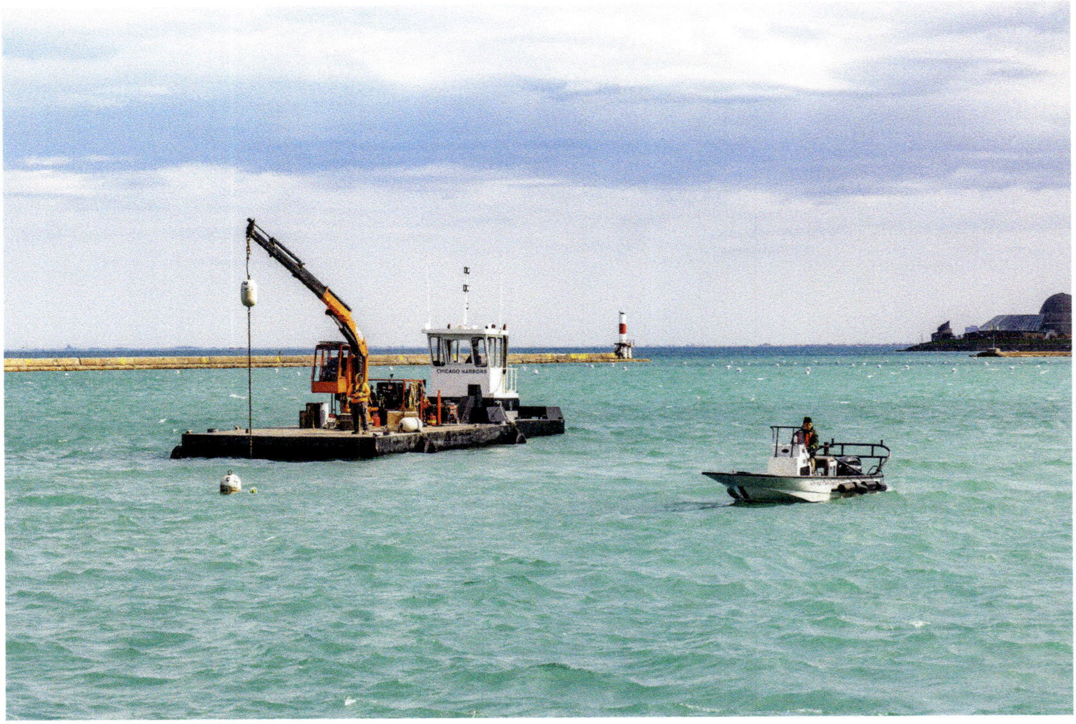

Deploying buoys at the start of the season in Monroe Harbor. April 2025.

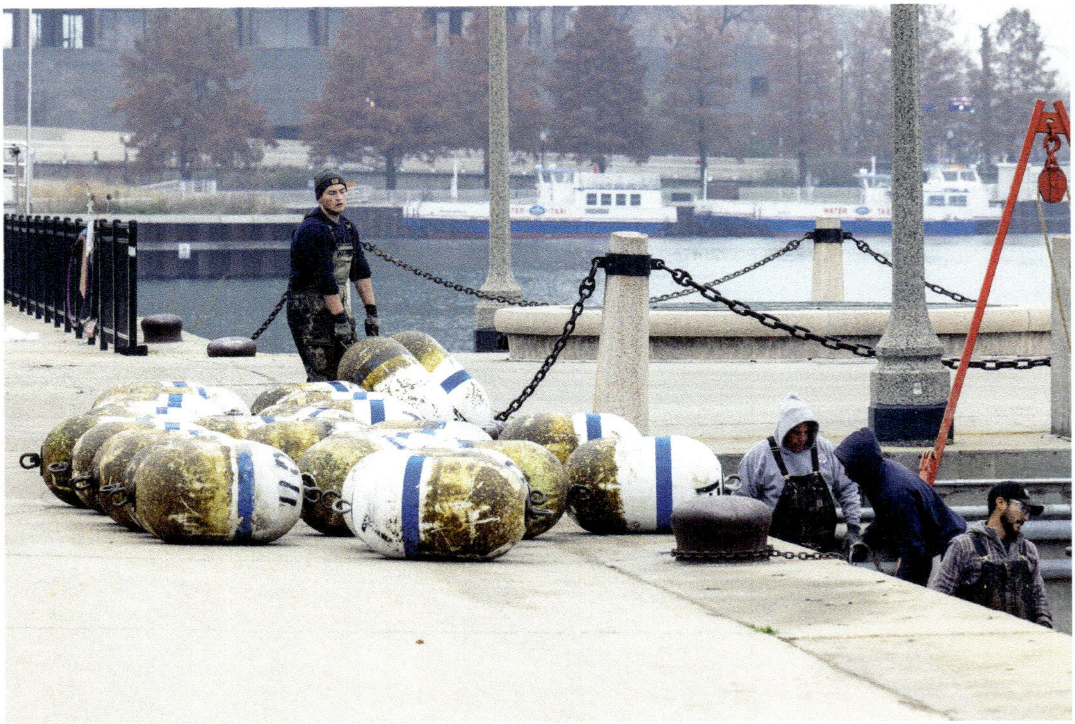

Unloading buoys at DuSable Harbor. November 2024.

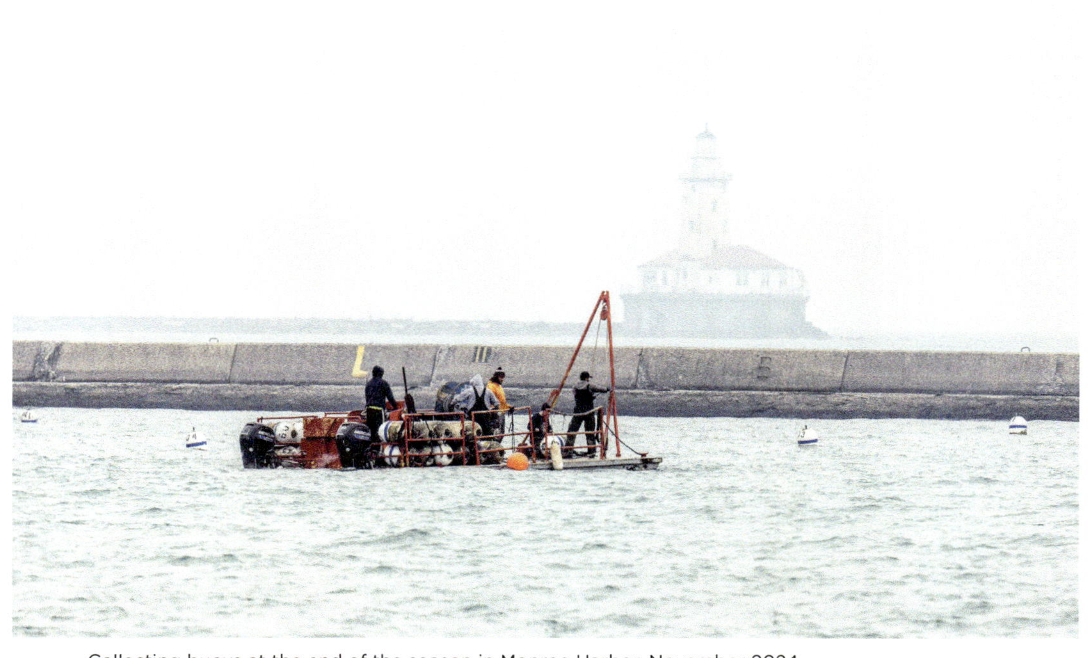

Collecting buoys at the end of the season in Monroe Harbor. November 2024.

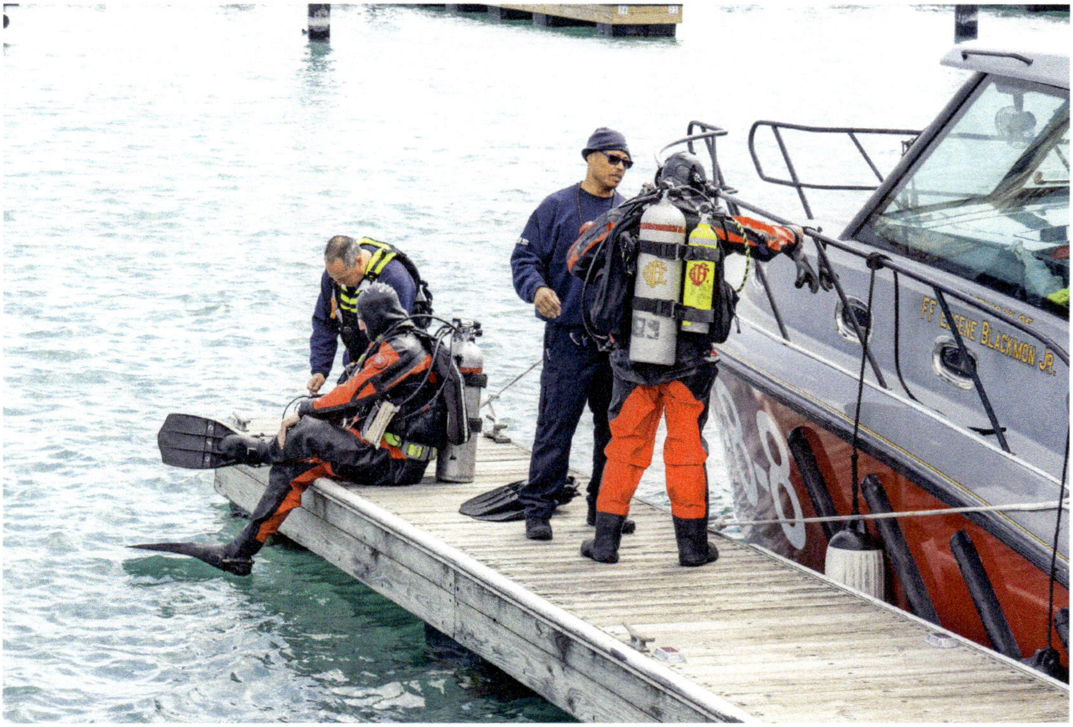

Air and Sea Rescue Unit, Chicago Fire Dept. DuSable Harbor. April 2025.

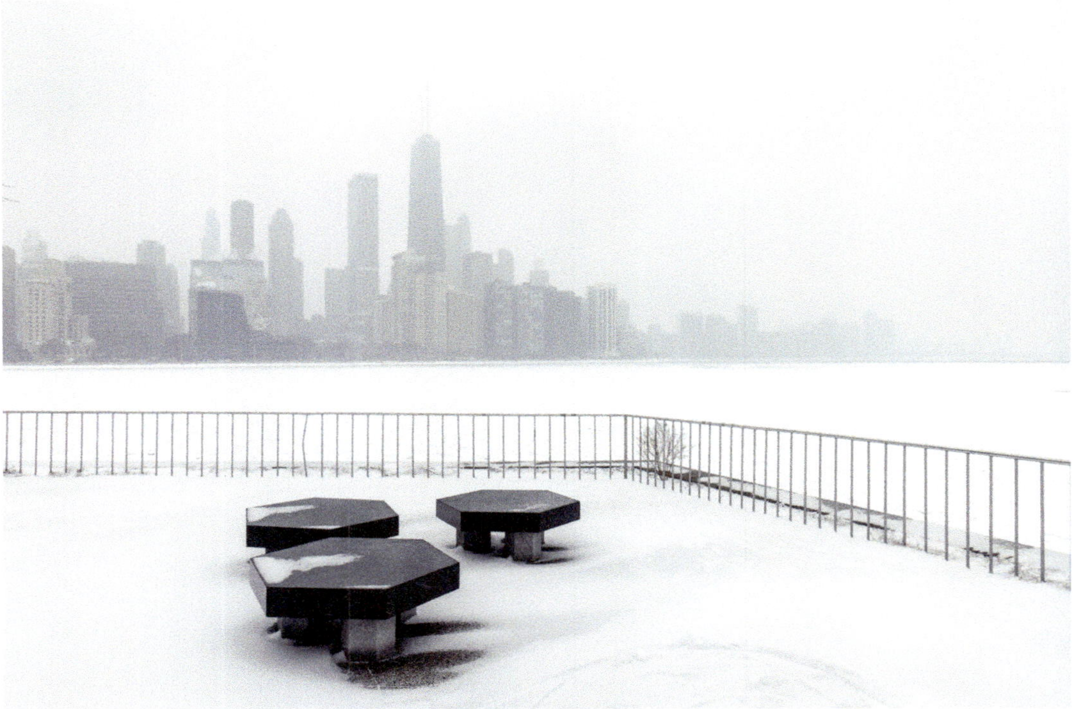

View from Milton Lee Olive Park. January 2025.

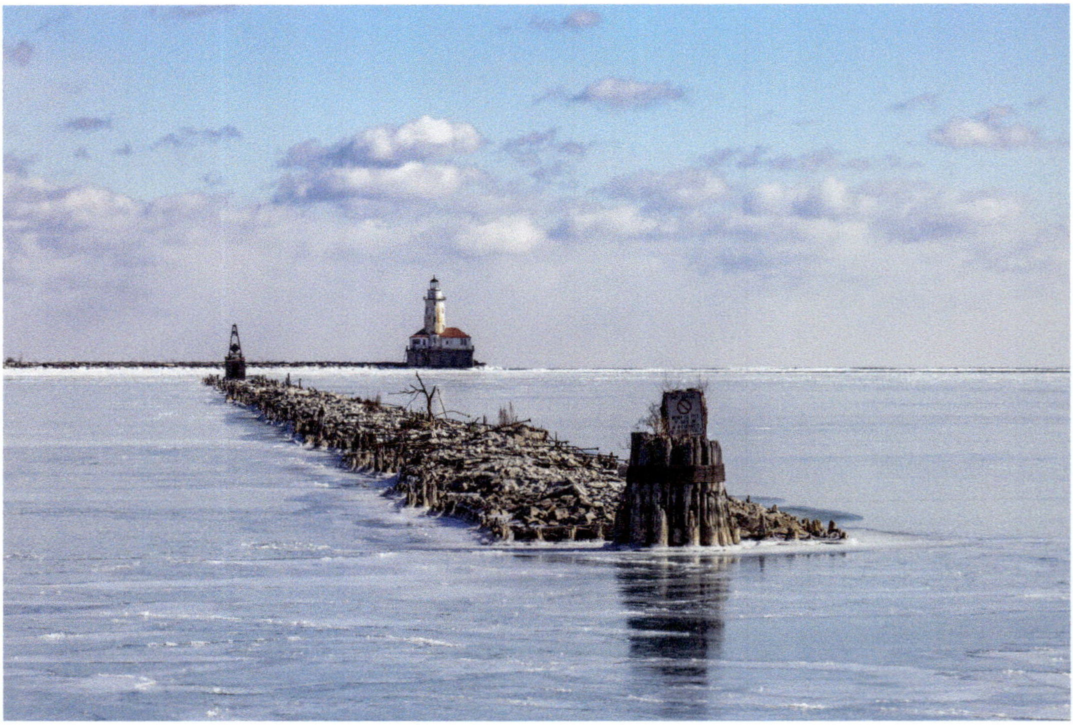

Breakwater and the Chicago Harbor Light. January 2025.

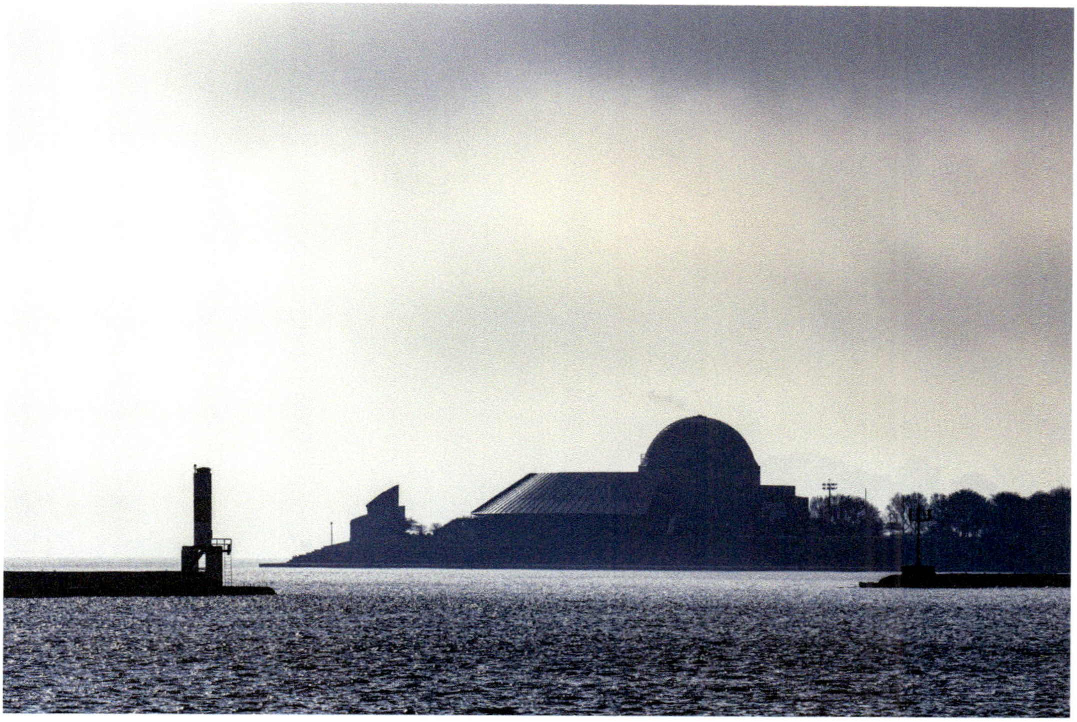

Adler Planetarium from Monroe Harbor. December 2024.

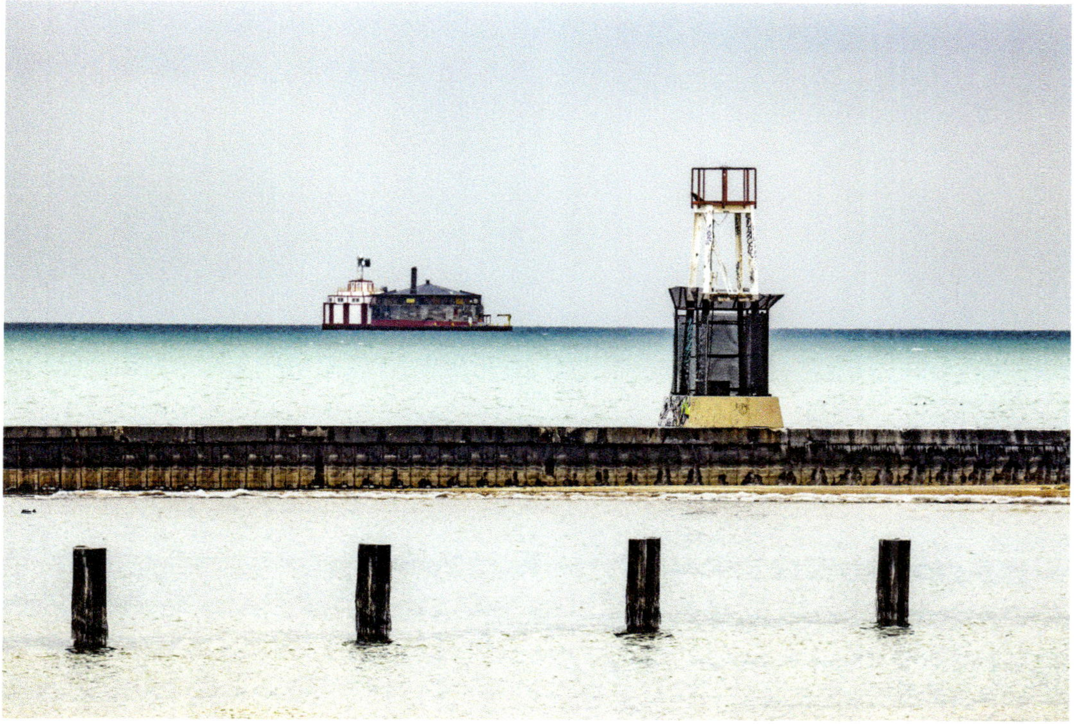

North Avenue Beach Pier and the William E. Denver Crib Lighthouse. December 2024.

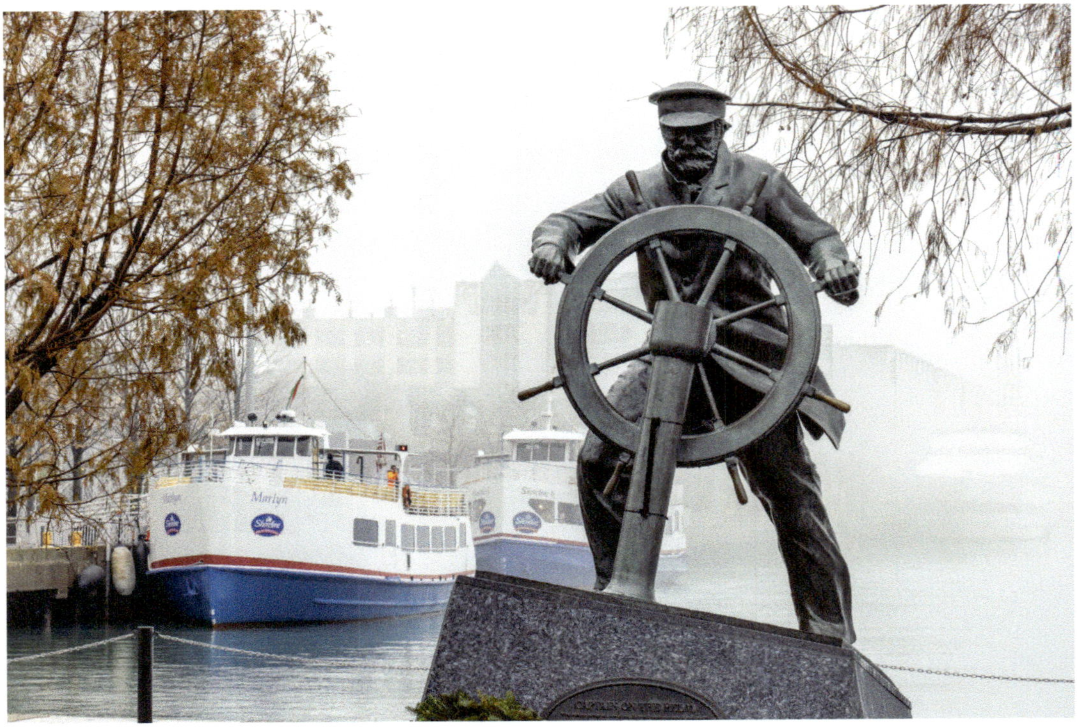

"Captain on the Helm." A sculpture at Navy Pier honoring Captain Streeter. December 2024.

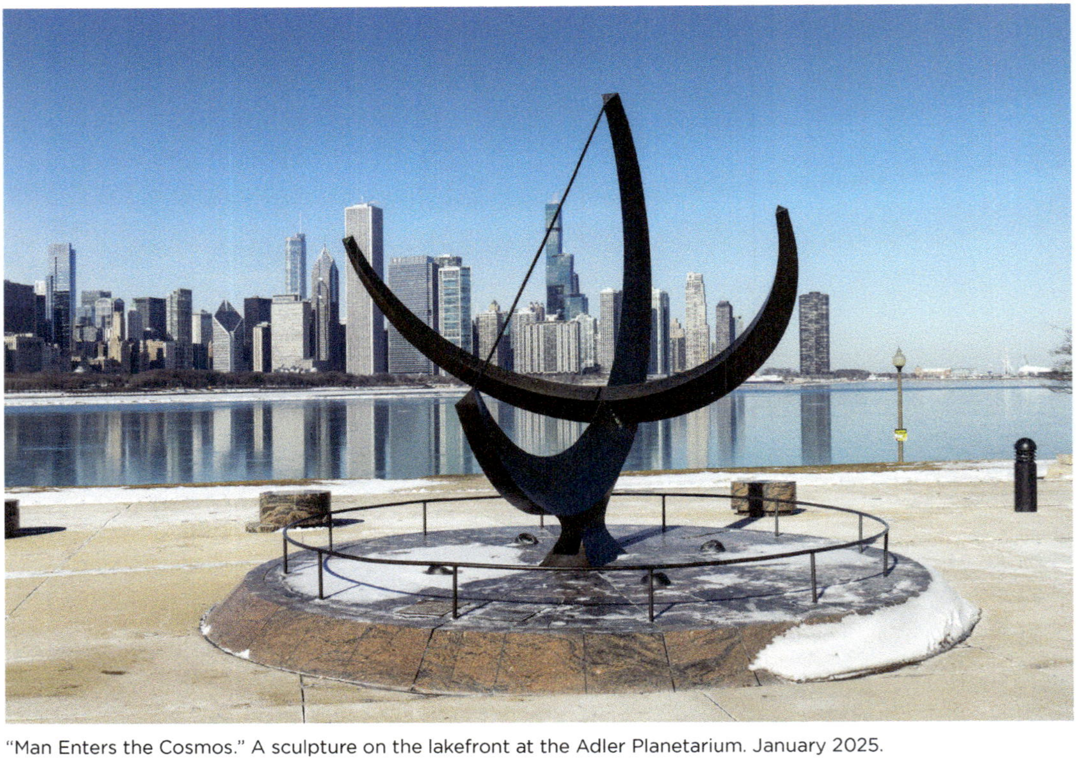

"Man Enters the Cosmos." A sculpture on the lakefront at the Adler Planetarium. January 2025.

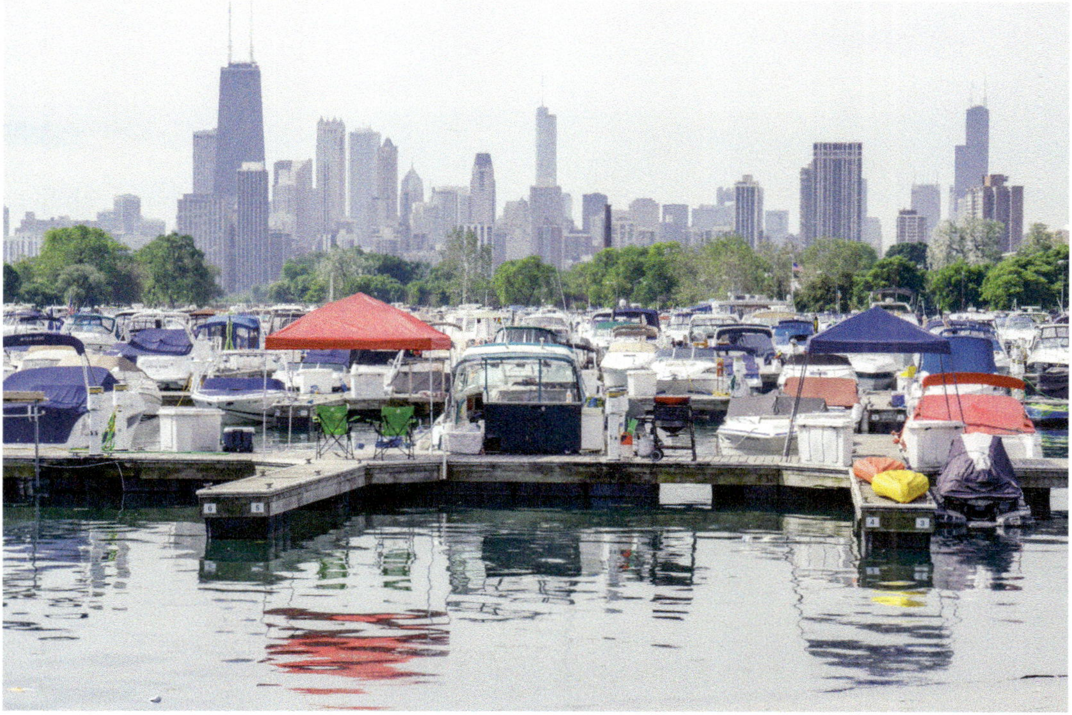

Above: Diversey Harbor in Lincoln Park. June 2014.

Right: The Lakefront Trail crossing the river on Lake Shore Drive Bridge. April 2025.

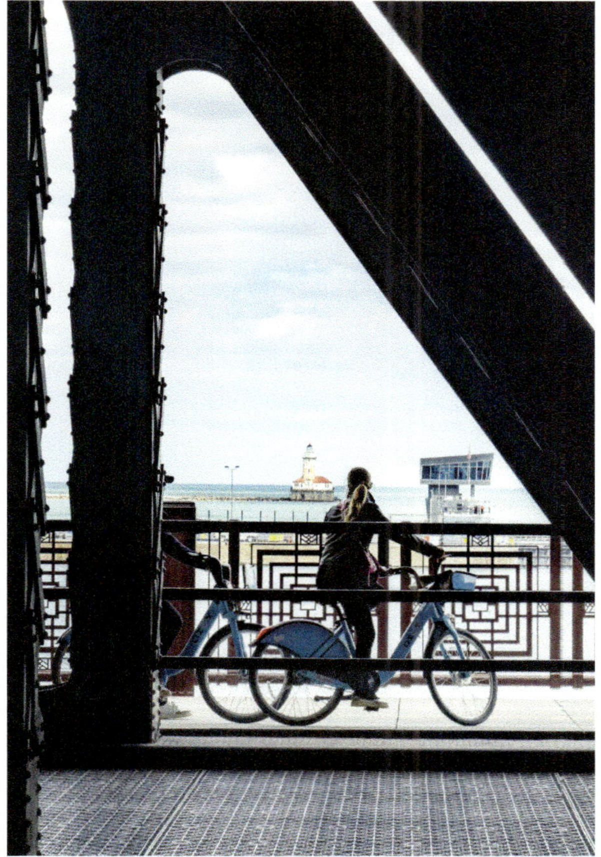

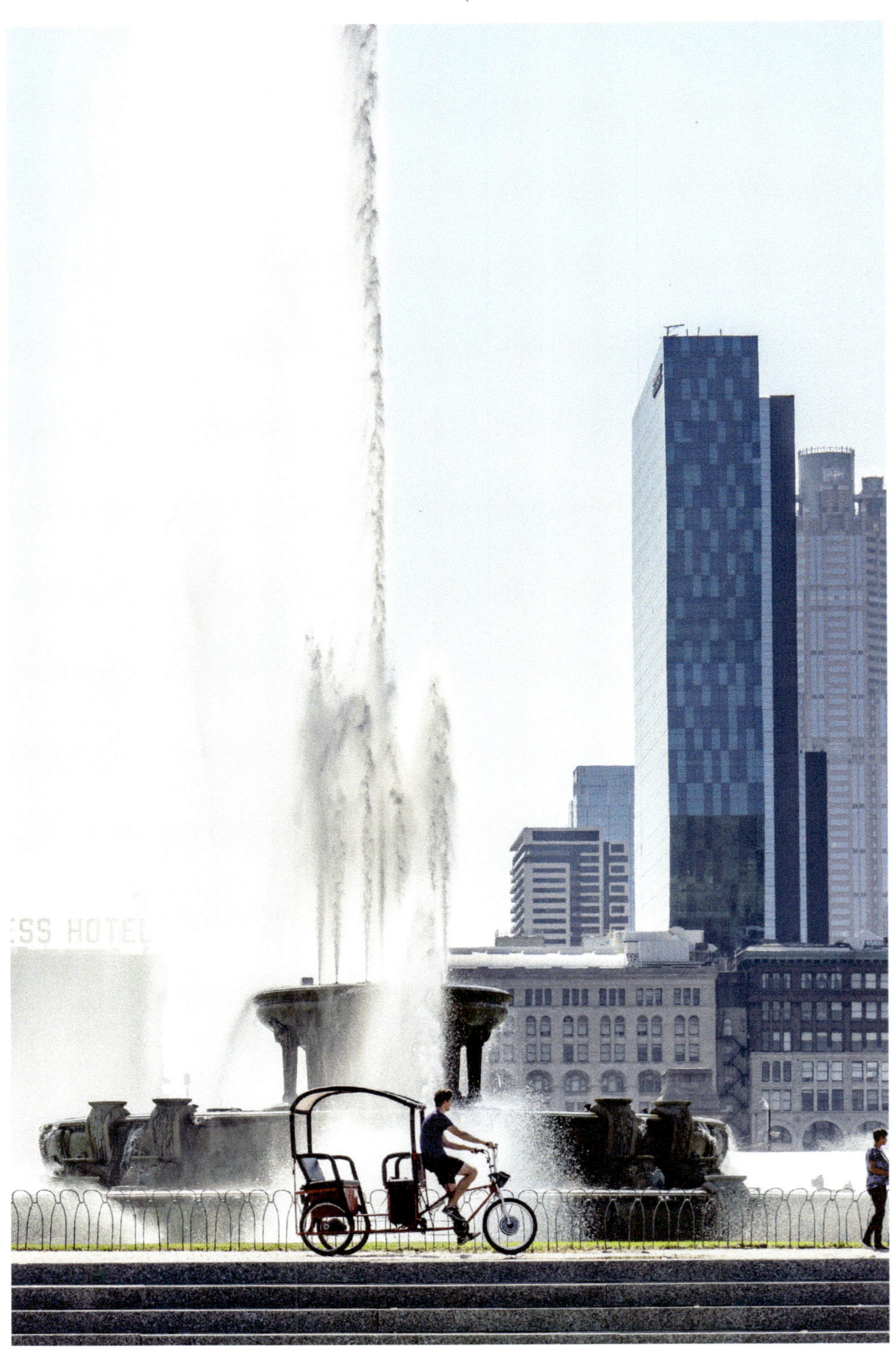

Clarence F. Buckingham Memorial Fountain in Grant Park. July 2022.

4
The Parks

When Chicago's motto "Urbs in horto – City in a garden" was adopted in 1837, Chicago was not much of a city and not in anything like a garden. However, in modern times Chicago, with its extensive park system, lives up to its motto. There are parks throughout the metropolitan area, but the main ones are along the lake: Lincoln Park on the north side, Grant Park in the Loop, and Jackson Park on the south side. A statue of President Grant presides over Lincoln Park, which is somewhat ironic since President Lincoln's statue presides over Grant Park.

Lincoln Park, the largest of the parks, stretches along the lakefront from Ohio Street Beach downtown to the far-north community of Edgewater. Just south of West Fullerton Avenue, the park contains the Alfred Caldwell Lily Pool, a hidden gem that has been designated a national historic landmark. Nearby, on a 35-acre site, is the Lincoln Park Zoo which was founded in 1868 and is the second oldest in the United States. It exhibits about 1,100 animals and is free, although if you have a car, you pay for parking. To the south there is a farm with pigs, cows, horses, and photogenic white barns. This "Farm-in-the-Zoo" was designed to "give Chicago Kids a chance to experience a bit of the country in the city." A Victorian-era glasshouse, the Lincoln Park Conservatory, is also located close to the zoo, at its northern end.

Grant Park extends along the lakefront east of Michigan Avenue. It contains Millenium Park and Maggie Daley Park; two relatively new sections connected by the BP Pedestrian Bridge across Columbus Drive. The key Grant Park attractions include Crown Fountain, Cloud Gate, the Lurie Garden, and the Pritzker Pavillion in the Millenium Park section, and to the South, the Clarence Buckingham Memorial Fountain.

Jackson Park is about 7 miles south of the Loop and is the site of the 1893 World's Columbian Exposition. Relics from this major World's Fair include the Museum of Science and Industry (which in 1893 was the Palace of Fine Arts) and Osaka Garden (also called the Garden of the Phoenix). This beautiful Japanese garden provides a quiet place for contemplation and is a hidden treasure worth visiting in all seasons. A new addition to Jackson Park, under construction at the time of writing, will be the Barack Obama Presidential Center.

There are other lakefront parks. Perhaps the most unusual is Steelworkers Park which is located in the far south, on the north bank of the Calumet River. The site was part of the U.S. Steel Complex known as South Works which closed in 1992. Much of it was built on landfill made of molten slag. The park retains remnants from its industrial history, notably a series of enormous parallel concrete ore walls which are now popular climbing features. For those interested in derelict things, at the bottom of one wall there is a room containing rusty lockers. At the northern edge of the park, the North Slip is a short canal which is popular with local anglers. If you ask, they will be happy to show you their catch and tell you about the one they caught yesterday.

In addition to the lakefront parks, there are also parks on the banks of the Chicago River. An example is Ping Tom Memorial Park which serves Chinatown. It features a pagoda-style pavilion where, early on summer mornings, you might see locals performing Tai Chi. The north part of the park has a boat house and a riverside walk with fine views of downtown Chicago. The Chicago Park District manages many other parks but not all of them are easy to get to. One accessible destination is the Garfield Park Conservatory which is on the Green Line of the L. The conservatory, which was built between 1906 and 1907, was designed by famed landscape architect Jens Jensen and collaborators. The large glass structures are designed to resemble the haystacks of the Midwest. The interior of the conservatory is sometimes referred to as "landscape art under glass."

Finally, for those who wish to visit some of the heroines and heroes from Chicago's past, there is the park-like Graceland Cemetery. Its residents include architects Louis Sullivan and Daniel Burnham, railway industrialist George Pullman, detective Allan Pinkerton, and many others. The cemetery is landscaped with trees and a lagoon and is particularly photogenic in the fall when the leaves turn color.

Photographer Tips

i) On the Great Lawn in Millennium Park, between May and August, there are free Saturday morning workouts which are fun to watch or even participate in.

ii) In the winter there are ice skating rinks in both Millenium Park and Maggie Daley Park with good viewing locations.

iii) The South Pond bridge in Lincoln Park provides good views of Chicago's skyline.

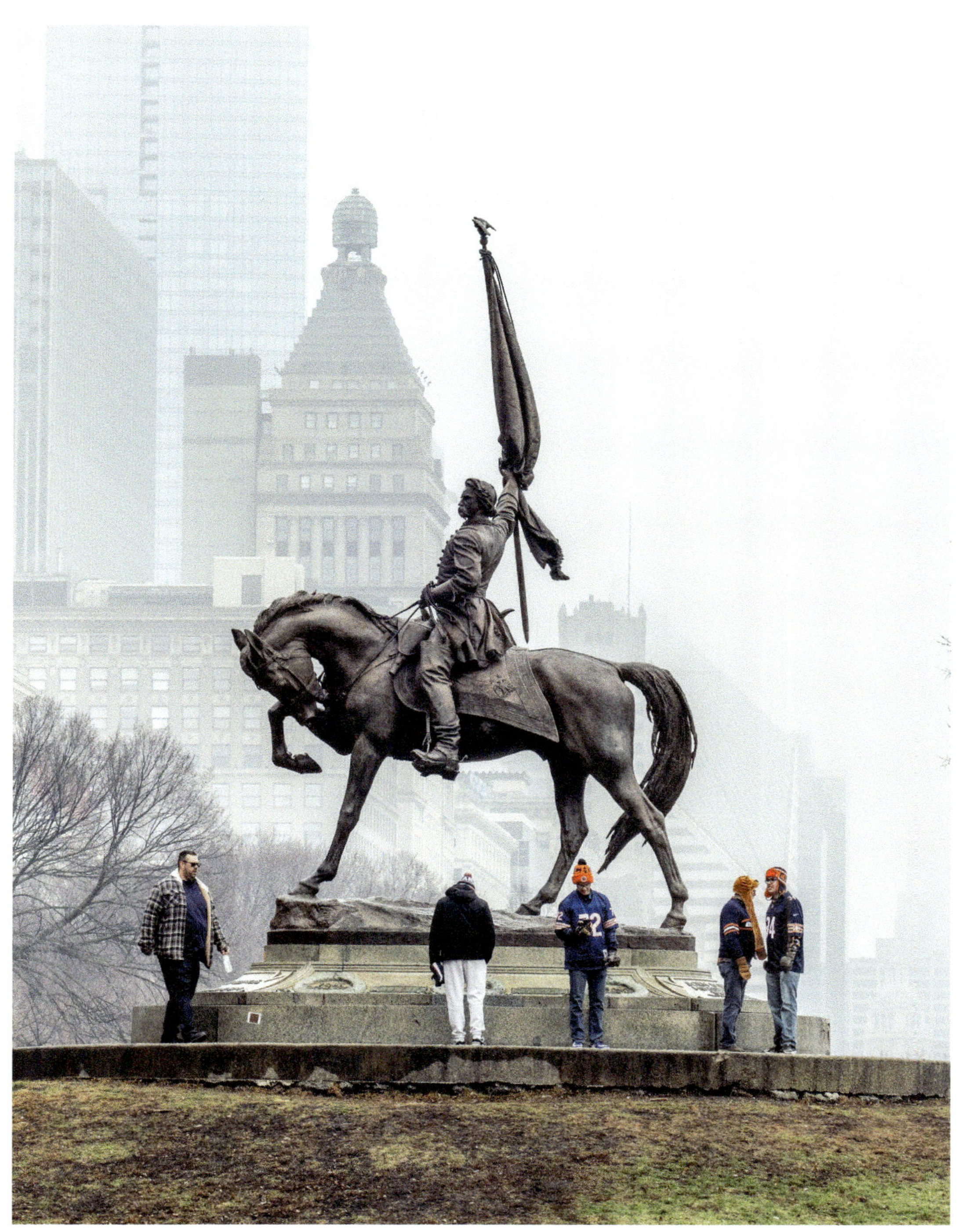

John Alexander Logan Monument in Grant Park. December 2024.

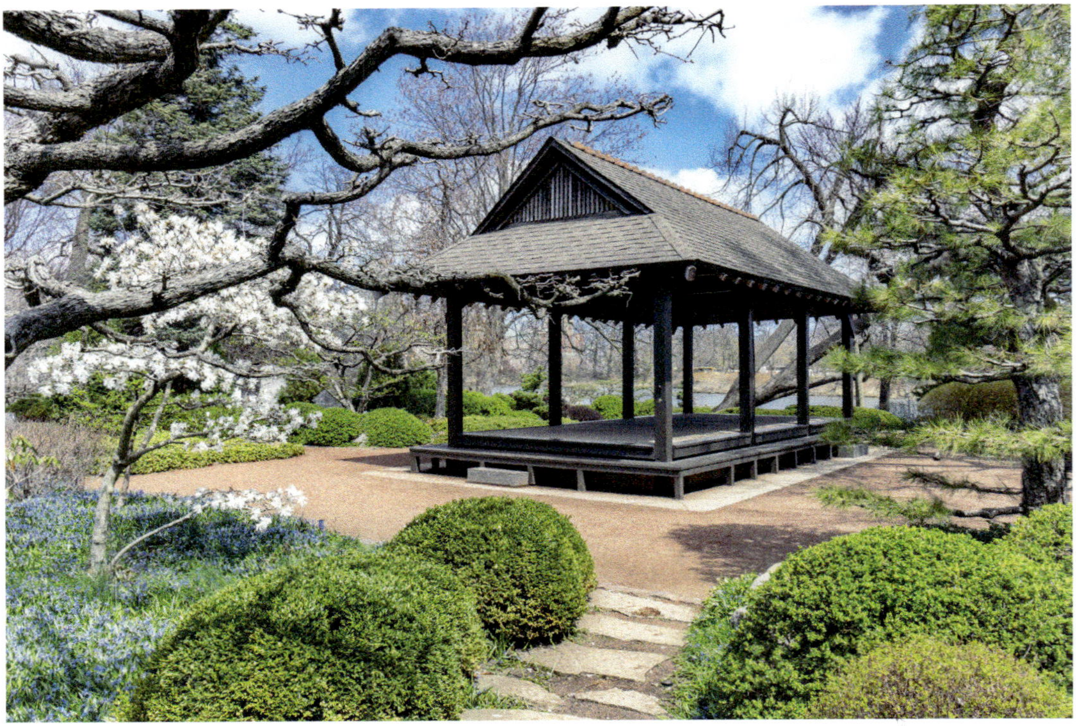

Osaka Garden (also called "Garden of the Phoenix") in Jackson Park. April 2025.

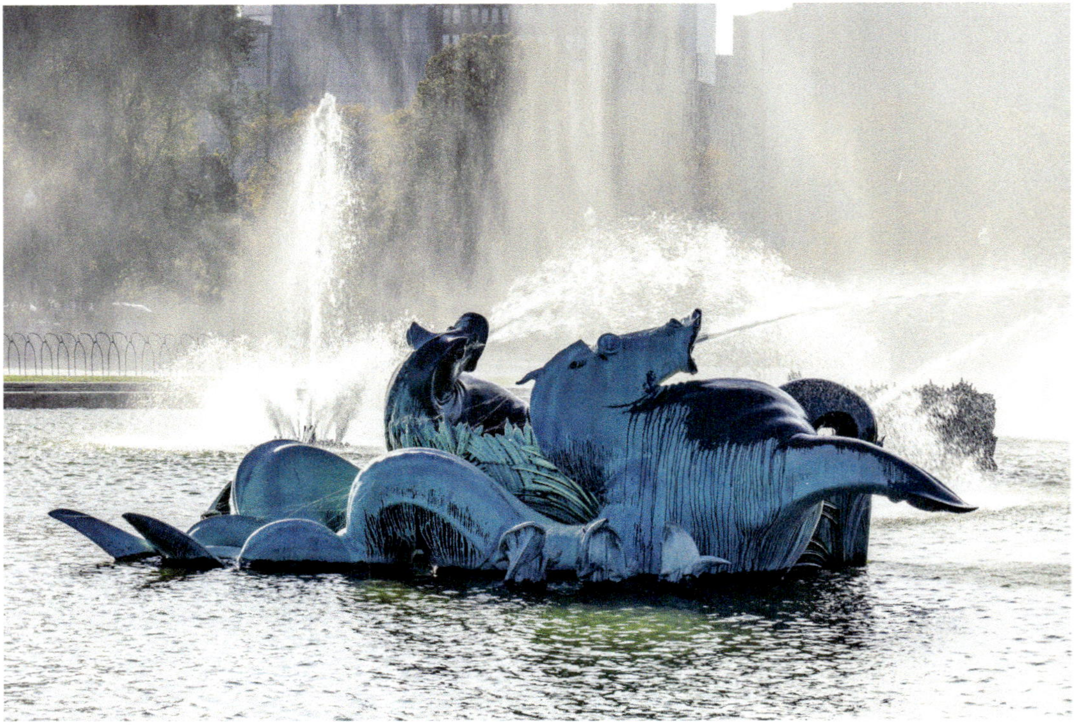

Clarence F. Buckingham Memorial Fountain in Grant Park. October 2024.

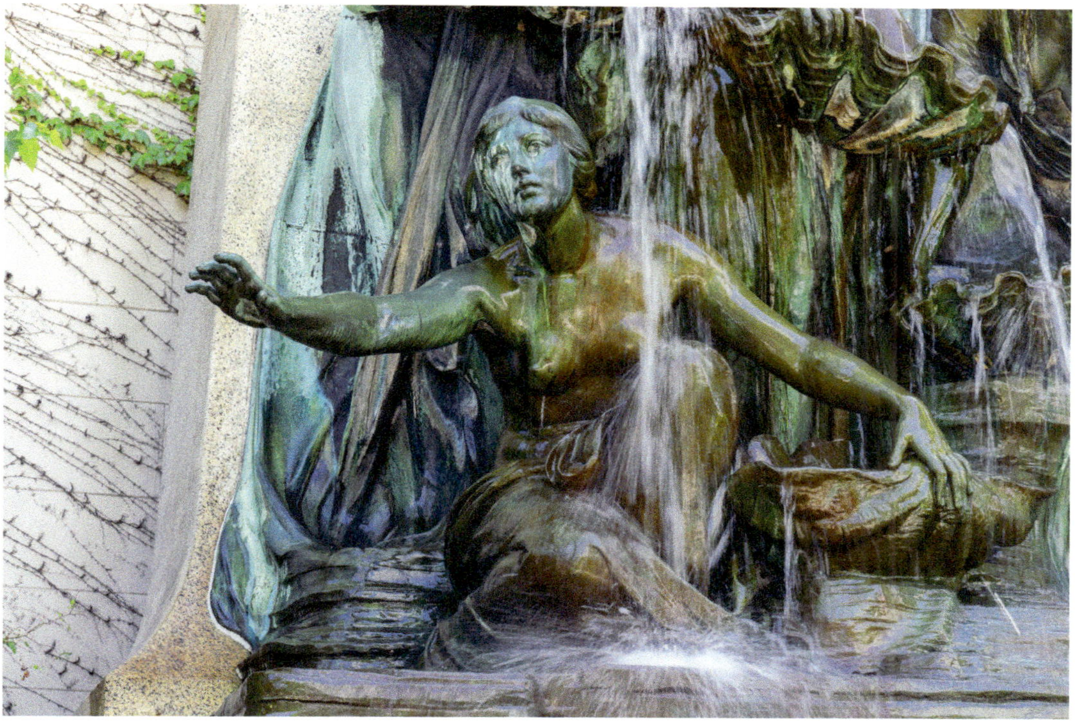

Fountain of the Great Lakes in the South Garden of the Art Institute of Chicago. June 2022.

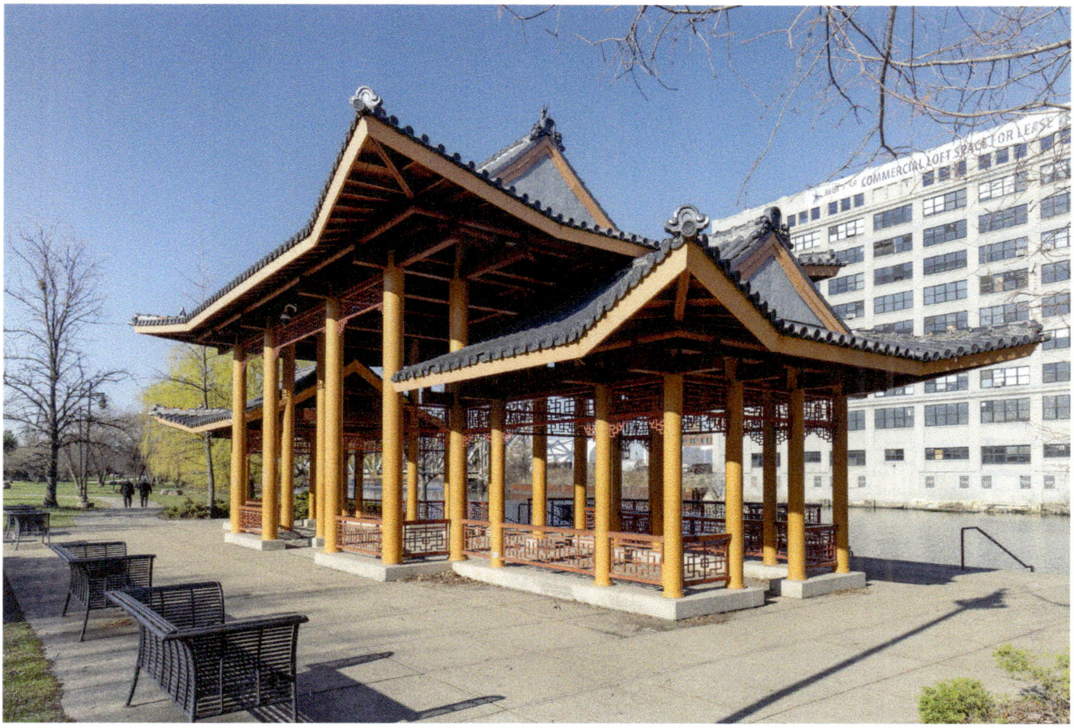

The Pagoda in Ping Tom Memorial Park. April 2025.

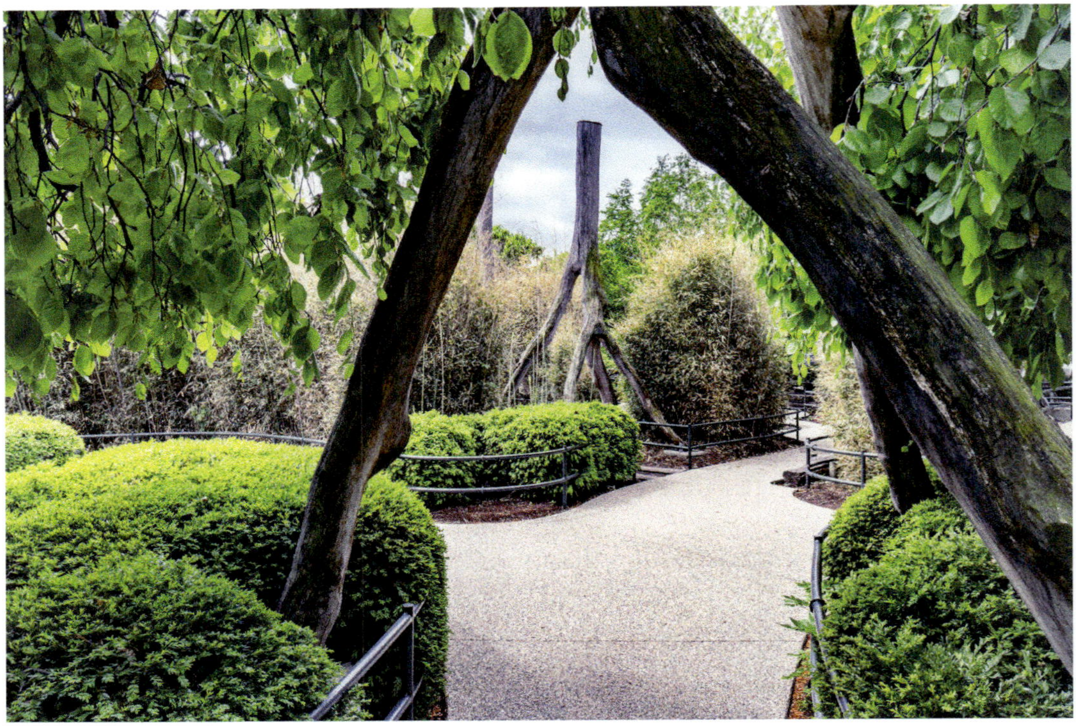

The Enchanted Forest in Maggie Daley Park. May 2025.

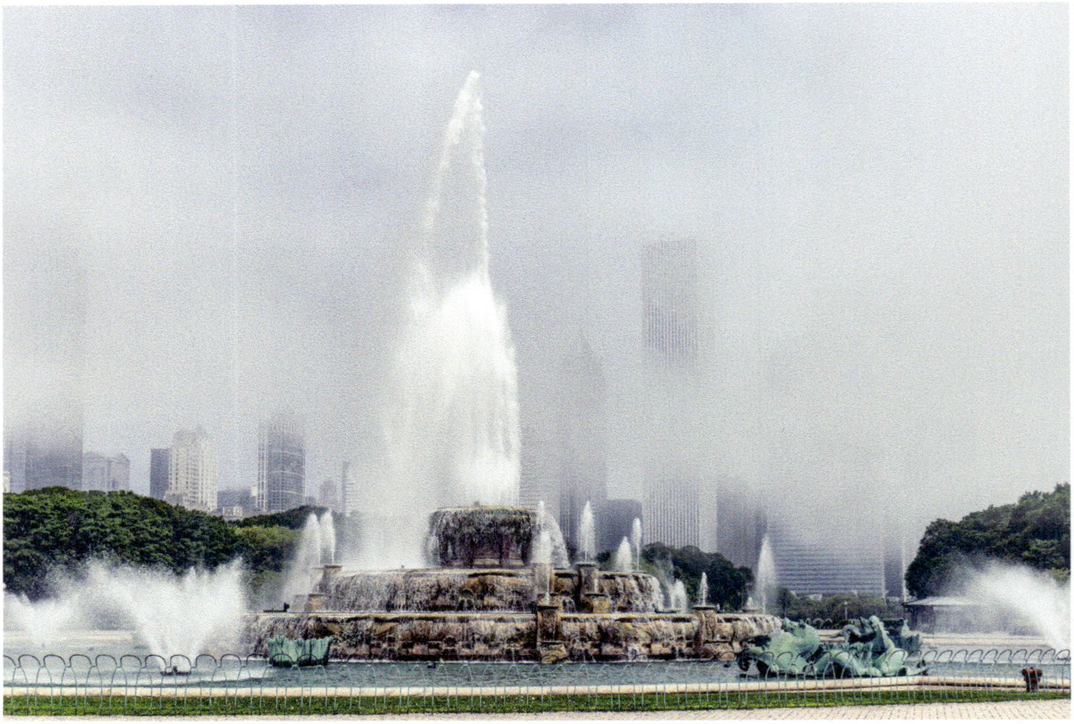

Clarence F. Buckingham Memorial Fountain in drifting lake-mist. May 2025.

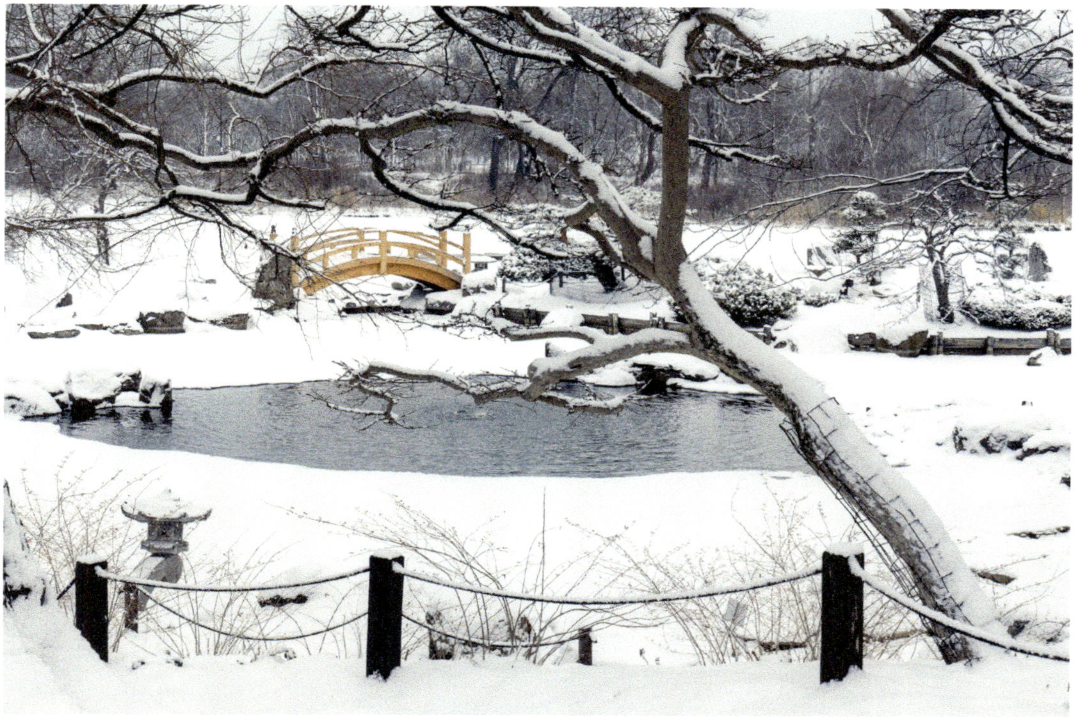

Osaka Garden in Jackson Park. January 2025.

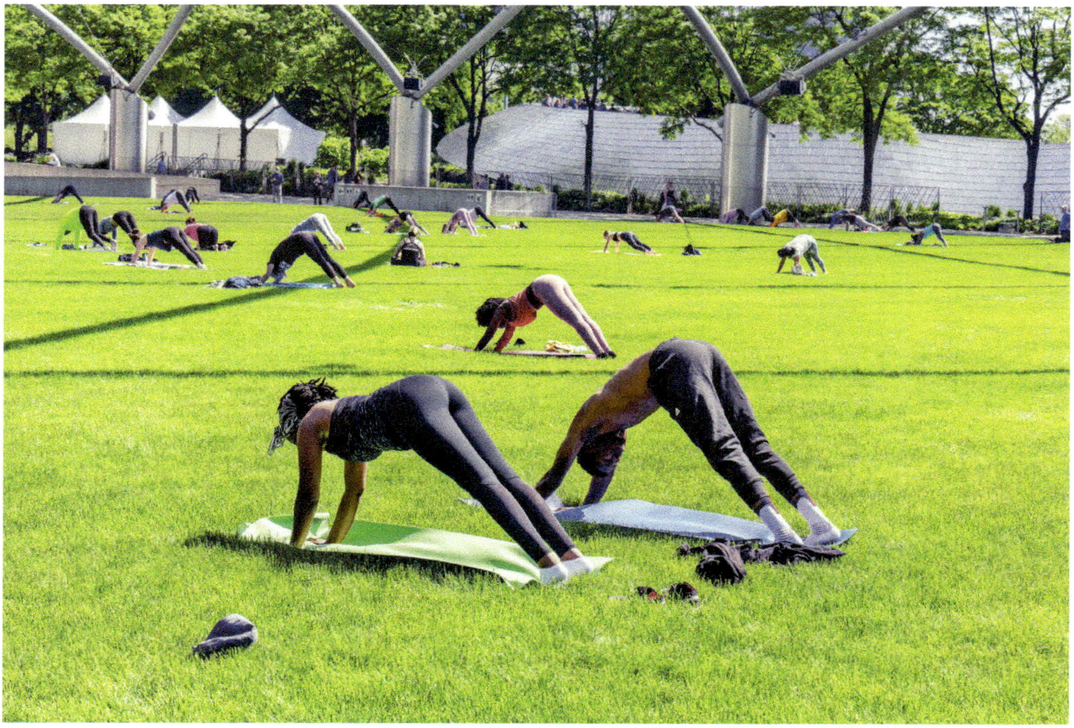

Saturday morning exercise class on The Great Lawn in Millennium Park. May 2022.

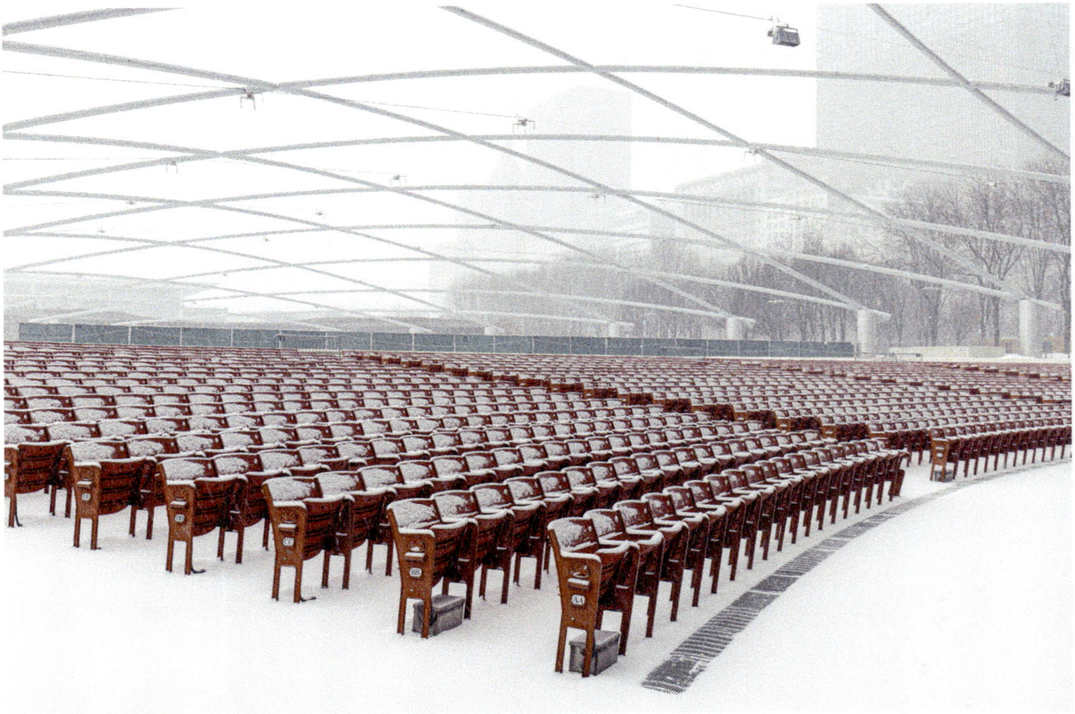

Jay Pritzker Pavilion in Millennium Park. February 2025.

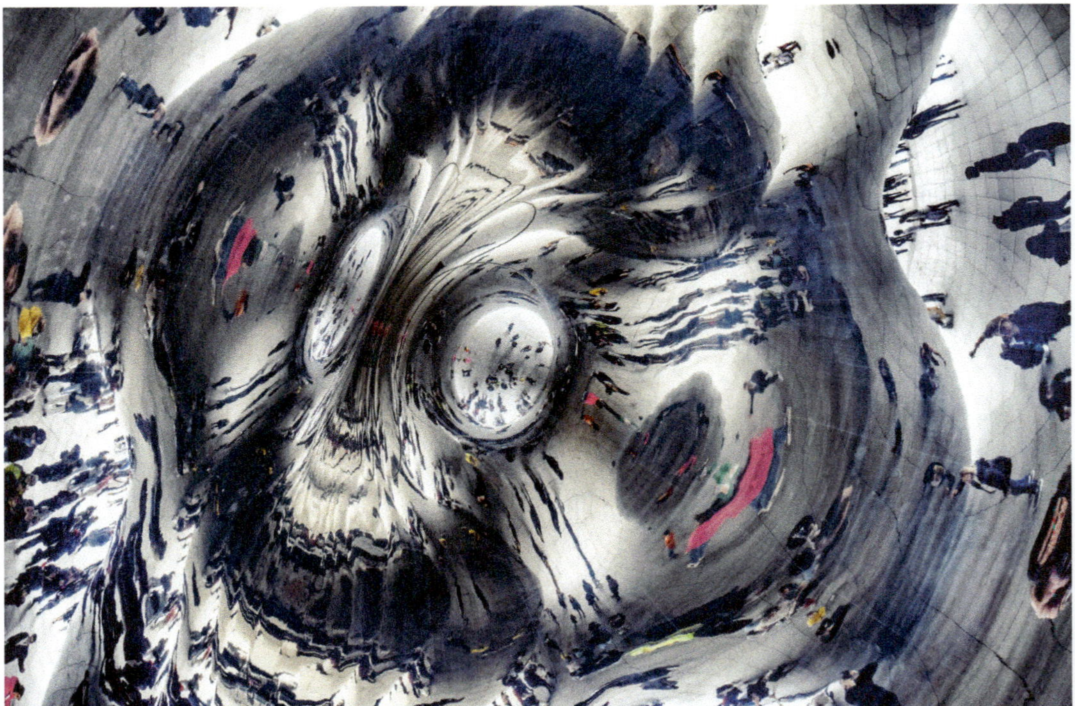

Cloud Gate in Millennium Park, viewed from below. April 2025.

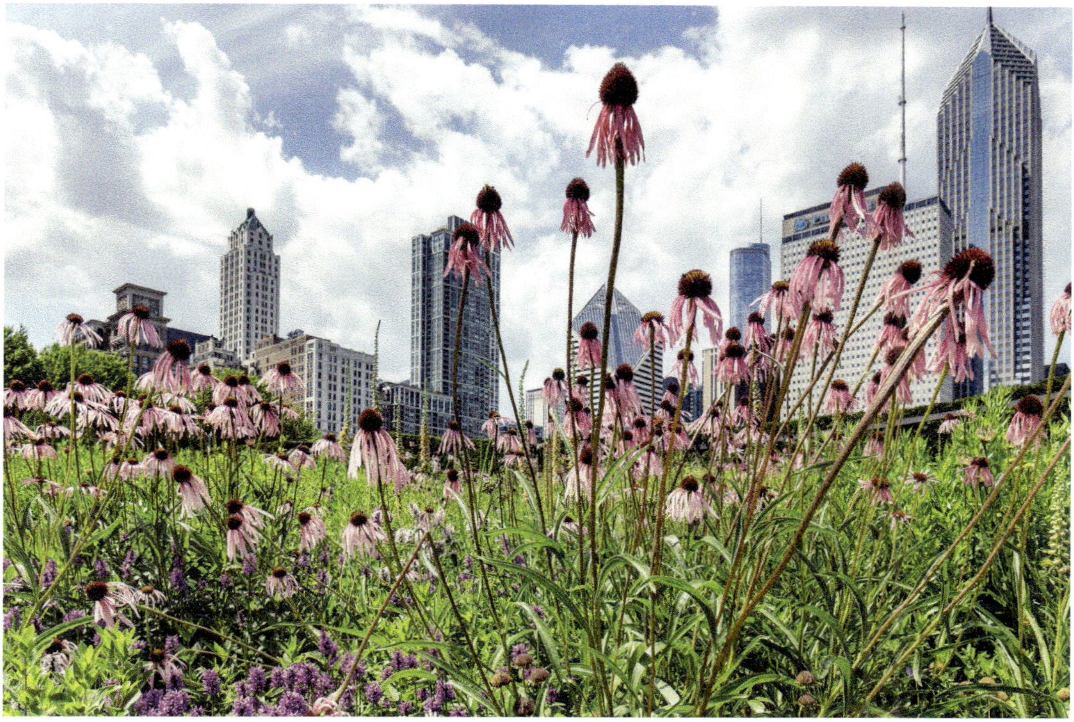

Lurie Garden in Millennium Park. June 2022.

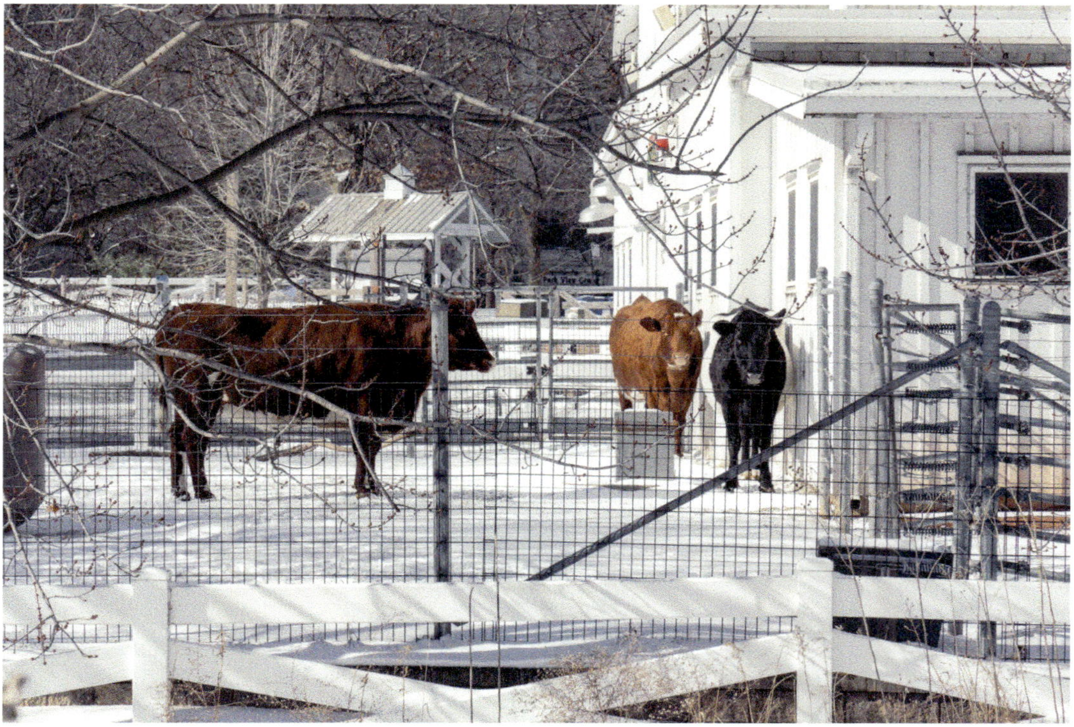

Farm-in-the-Zoo in Lincoln Park. February 2025.

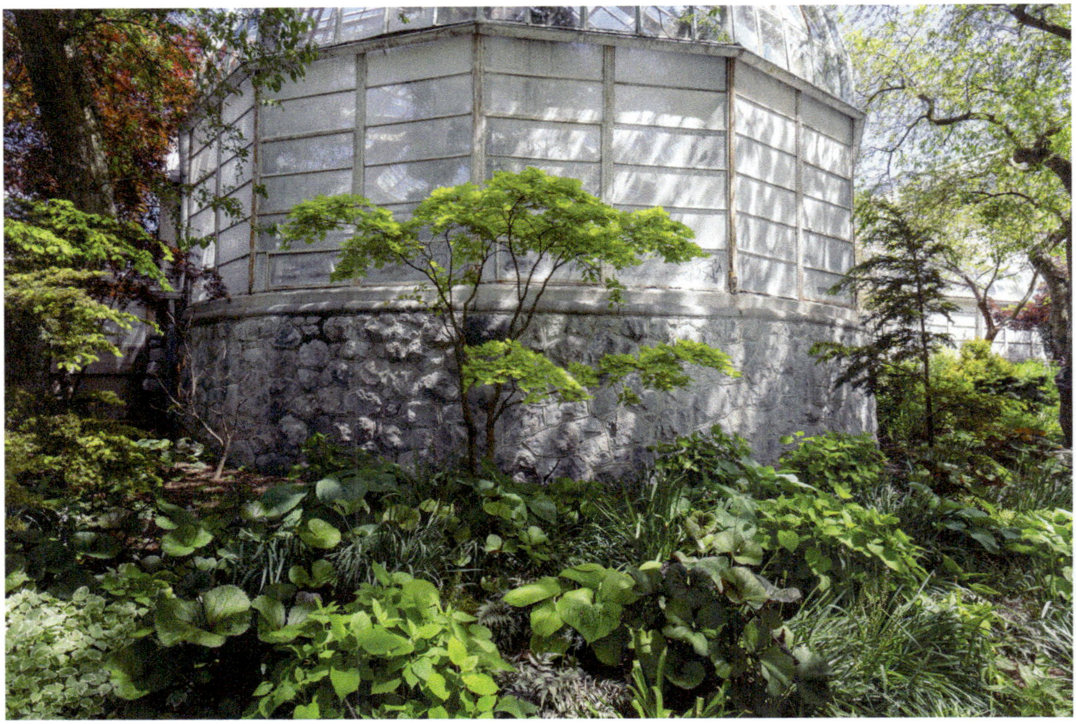

Lincoln Park Conservatory. May 2024.

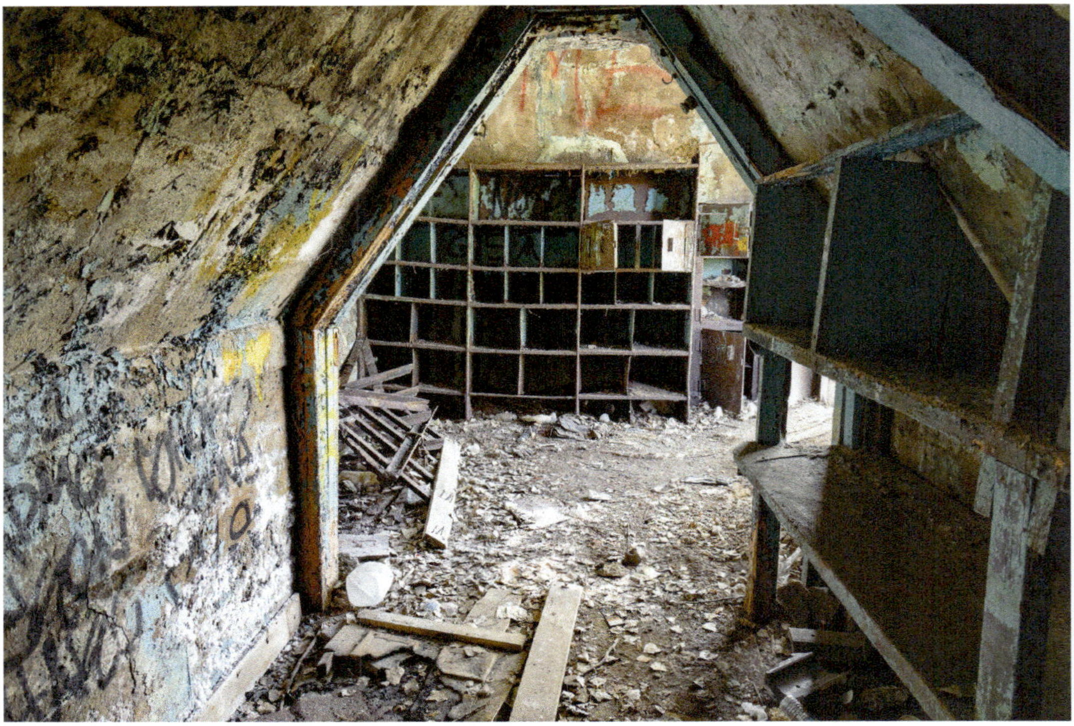

Locker room in the Steelworker's Park. February 2025.

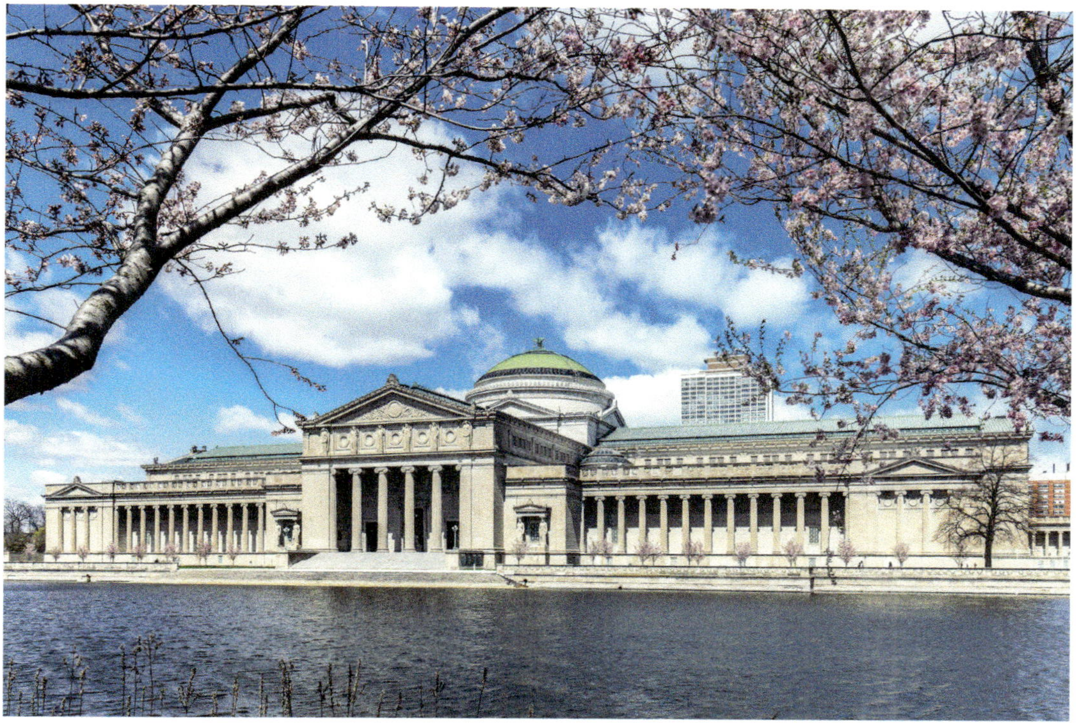

Cherry blossoms and the Museum of Science and Industry in Jackson Park. April 2025.

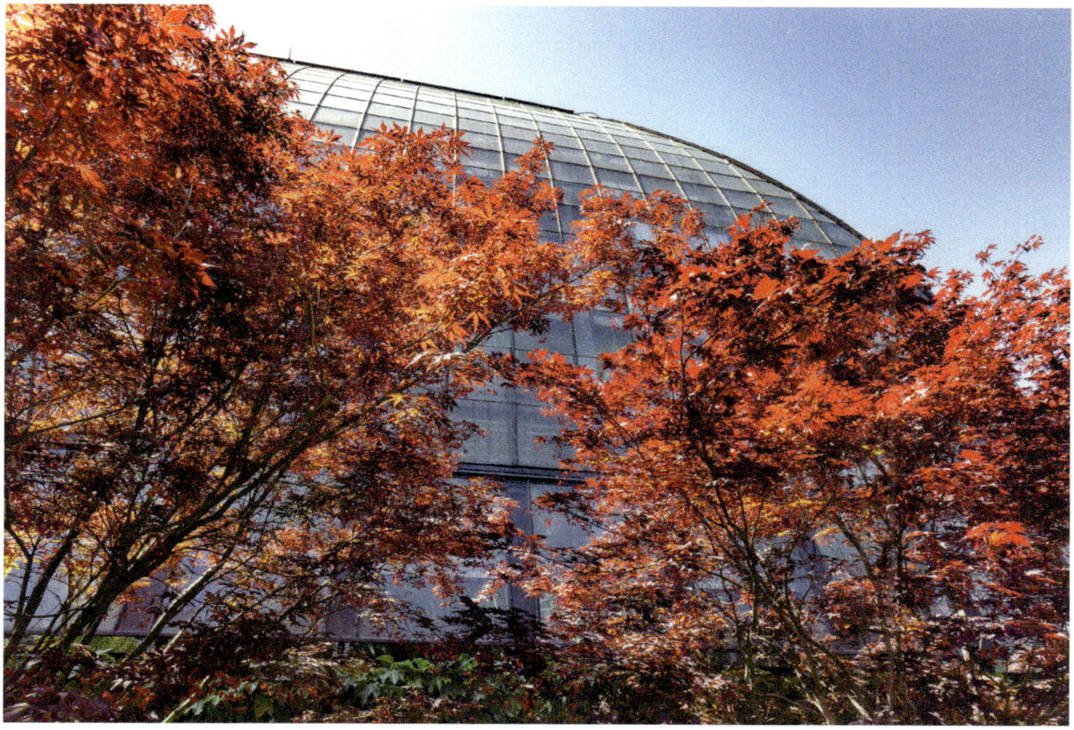

Garfield Park Conservatory. May 2025.

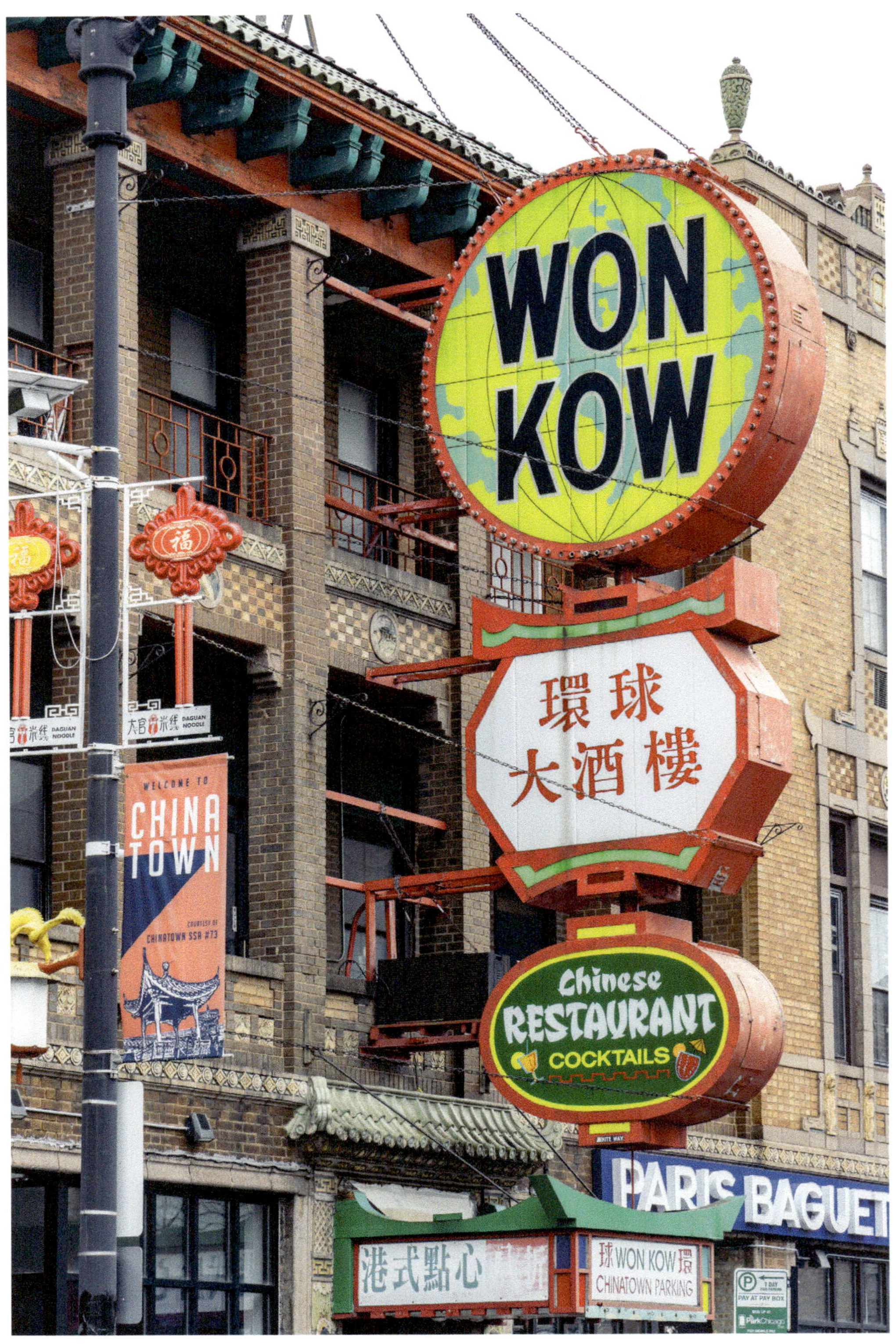

South Wentworth Avenue in Chinatown. April 2025.

5
Other Places

Only half of downtown Chicago is in the Loop. The other half is centered on the Magnificent Mile, which is the continuation of Michigan Avenue north of the river. At its southern end, two historic buildings built in the 1920s form a gateway to this roughly one-mile-long shopping street: the white terra-cotta-faced Wrigley Building and the neo-Gothic *Tribune* Tower. The walls of the Tribune Tower incorporate fragments from more than 150 famous buildings from around the world including, for example, the Houses of Parliament in London, the Great Pyramid of Giza in Egypt, and the Mosque of Suleiman the Magnificent in Istanbul. Towards the northern end of the Magnificent Mile there is another Chicago landmark, the Gothic Revival fairy-tale-like Chicago Water Tower. Built in 1869, it miraculously survived the Great Chicago Fire of 1871. On the other side of the street, you can visit the Chicago Avenue Pumping Station and see the infrastructure designed to pump water from the offshore water cribs in Lake Michigan. Two blocks to the north, the Tudor-style courtyard of the Fourth Presbyterian Church offers a quiet respite from the bustle of Michigan Avenue, or to completely escape from the shops, at the end of the Magnificent Mile there is an underpass that goes under Lake Shore Drive to the lakefront.

Beyond the Magnificent Mile, the Loop, the parks, the river and lake, there are many other places to explore, both near and far from downtown. Right next to the downtown area, on the lakefront at the southern end of Grant Park, a cluster of museums has been built on land slightly elevated above the lake. This is the Museum Campus, home to the Field Museum of Natural History, the John G. Shedd Aquarium, and the Adler Planetarium. It is also adjacent to Soldier Field, home of the Chicago Bears. On game days, a river of people flows through Grant Park and the Museum Campus to the stadium.

Further from the downtown area, Chicago is a city of neighborhoods. Some of them have a distinctive ethnic flavor. Chinatown is one of the most colorful and most visited.

Located 2.4-miles from the center of the Loop, it is easy to get to on the L or by water taxi (between May and September) and is home to more than one-third of Chicago's Chinese population. One of the two main areas in Chinatown for tourists to visit is located along Wentworth Avenue, from Cermak Road to 24th Place. It is a street of Chinese-themed gift-shops, grocery stores, and restaurants offering authentic cuisine. Wentworth Avenue is nearly always busy and during weekends in the summer it tends to be crowded. At the Cermak Road end of Wentworth Avenue there is Chinatown Gate and the ornately decorated Pui Tak Center (previously the On Leong Merchants Association Building) which was designated a Chicago Landmark in 1993. To the north, not far from Chinatown Gate, Chinatown Square is the second of the main visitor spots in Chinatown. It is centered on a plaza that has twelve large bronze zodiac figures. Next to the plaza, a two-story outdoor mall has many Chinese-themed shops and restaurants.

There are many other ethnic neighborhoods that are fun to visit. A short incomplete list will give a sense of their variety: Greektown, Bronzeville (African-American), Pilsen and Little Village (Mexican), Little India, Ukrainian Village, Little Italy, Humboldt Park (Puerto Rican), the Polish Triangle, Andersonville (Swedish), and Lincoln Square (German).

For the student of Chicago history, the site of the O'Leary barn on DeKovan Street is a place of special significance. One mile west of the lake, this is where the 1871 Great Fire of Chicago started. None of the combustible structures in DeKovan Street survived, but the site is marked by the Pillar of Fire, a modernist monument. It is also the location of the Chicago Fire Academy which has a display of various firefighting equipment including an old fire engine. Another place of historical interest is the Pullman Historic District which became a national park in 2015 and is located on the far south side of Chicago, about a thirty-minute drive from the Loop. Pullman was one of the first planned industrial communities in the United States. The historic district includes the site of the former Pullman Palace Car Works shops and administration building, the Hotel Florence, Arcade Park, the Greenstone Church, a museum, and several streets of workers' houses.

Photographer Tips

i) Chinatown and many of the other ethnic neighborhoods are good for street photography.
ii) Throughout Chicago there are service alleys between the streets. They provide photographic opportunities ranging from puddle reflections to documentary details.
iii) Many neighborhoods have interesting architecture. For example, near the Loop, Prairie Avenue is walkable and has landmark nineteenth-century mansions. To the north, Uptown has ornate terra-cotta-clad commercial buildings.

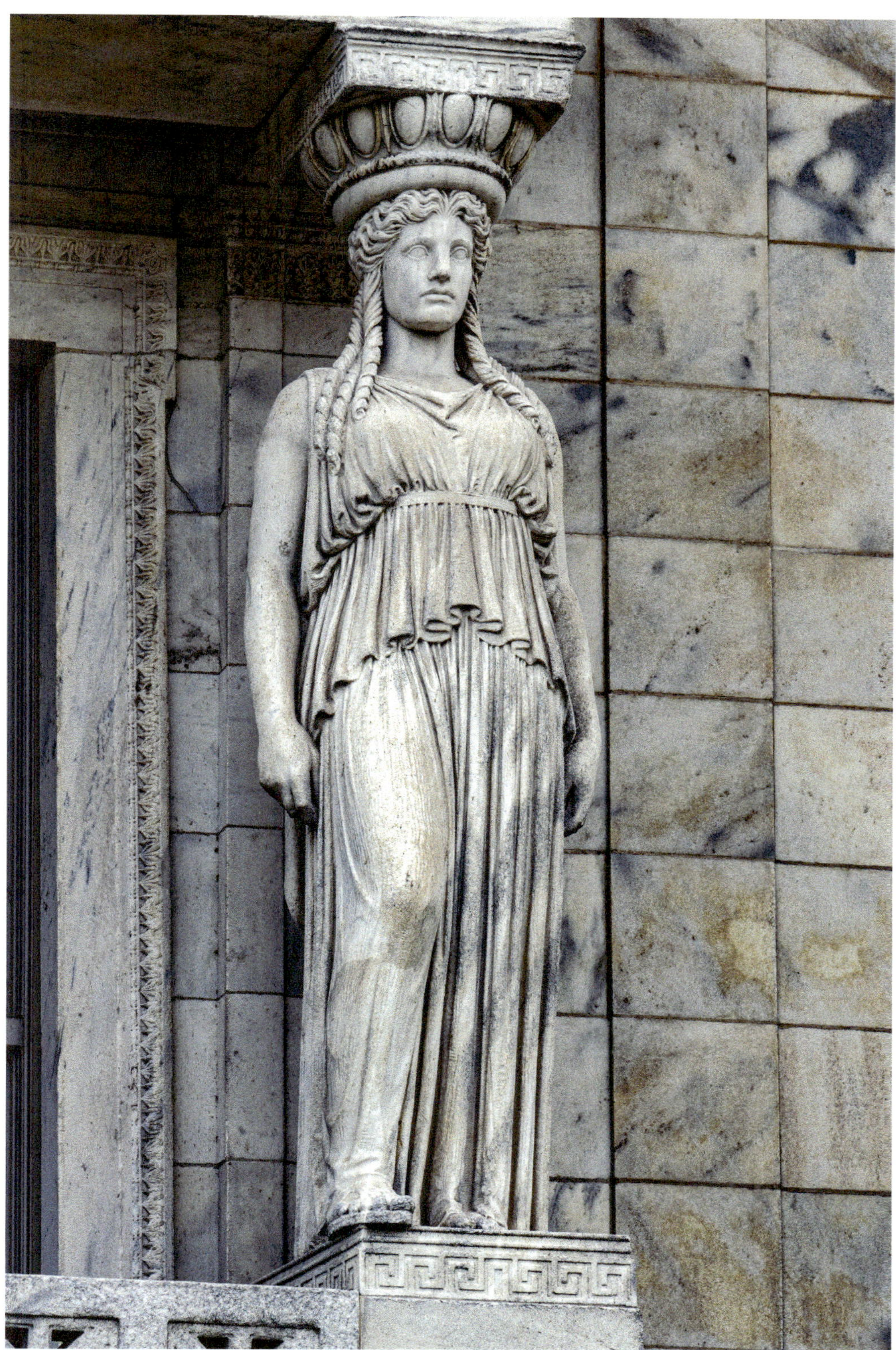

Caryatid decorating the Field Museum. May 2025.

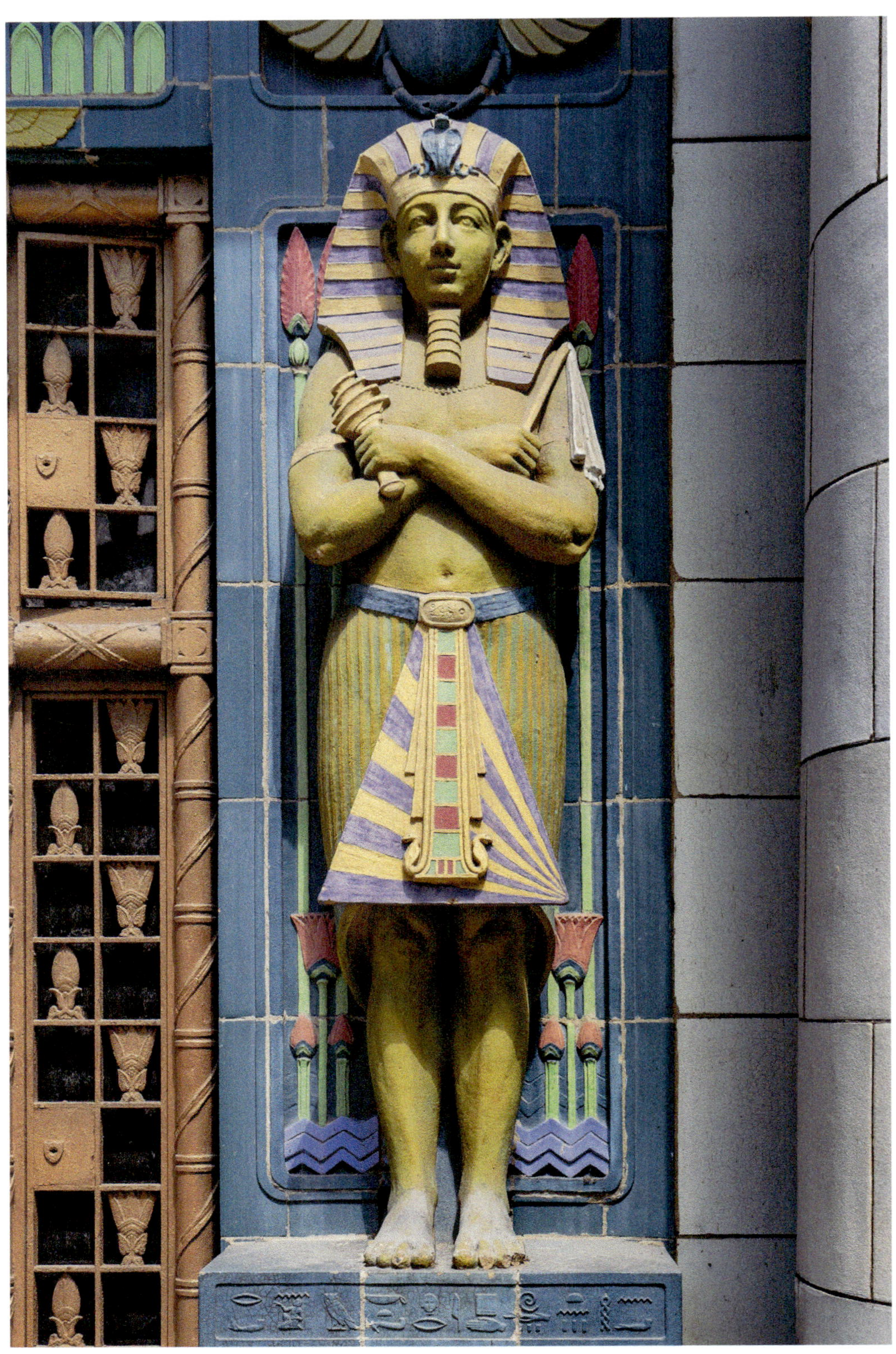

Ramses II guarding the Reebie Storage Warehouse in the Lincoln Park neighborhood. May 2025.

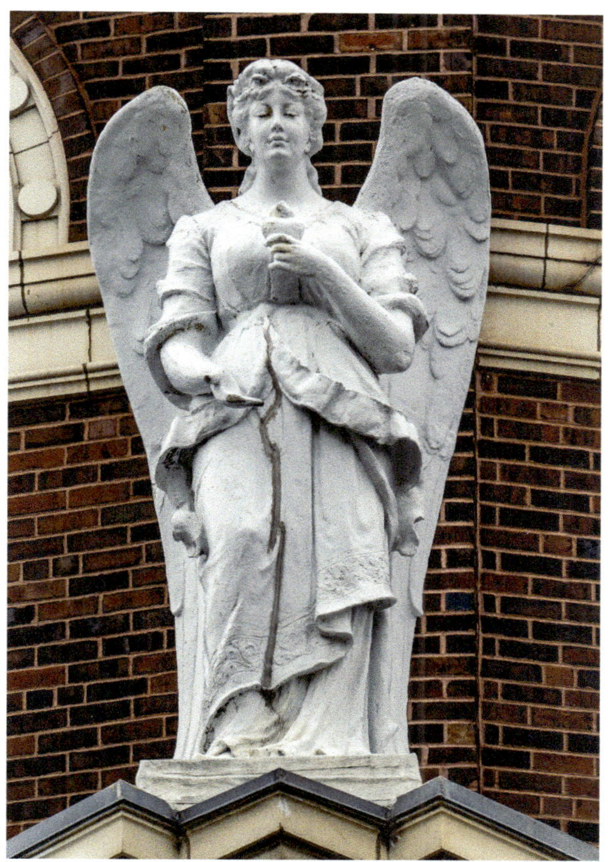

Right: St. Mary of the Angels in the Logan Square community area. May 2025.

Below: Tribune Tower reflected in the windows of 500 Lake Shore Drive. March 2014.

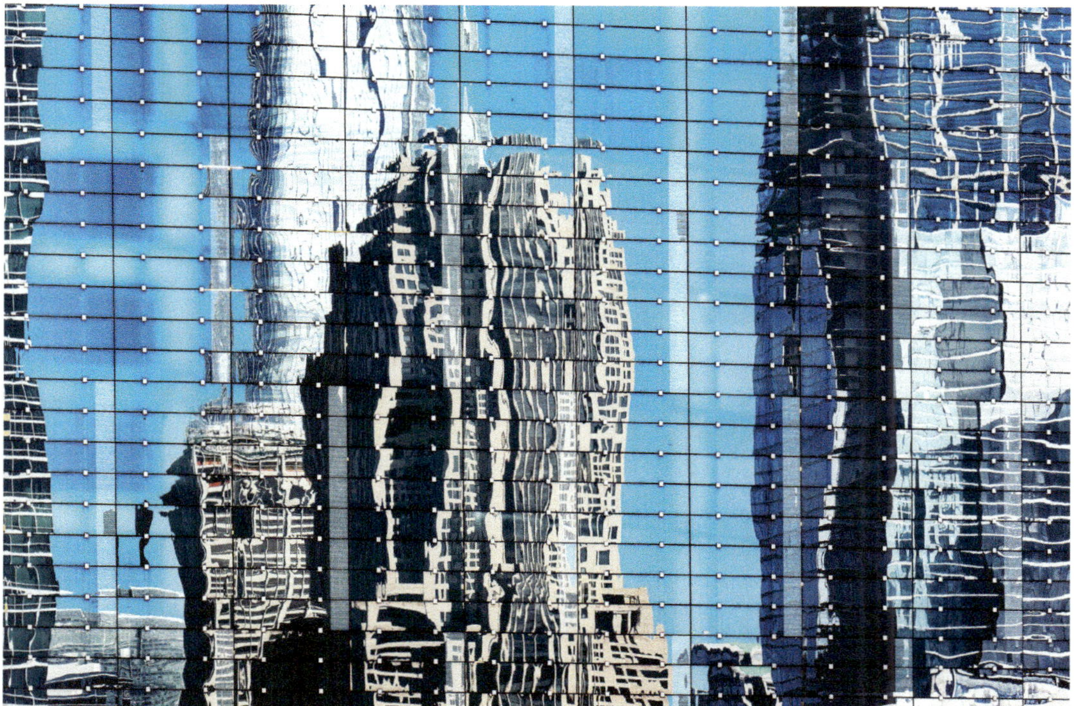

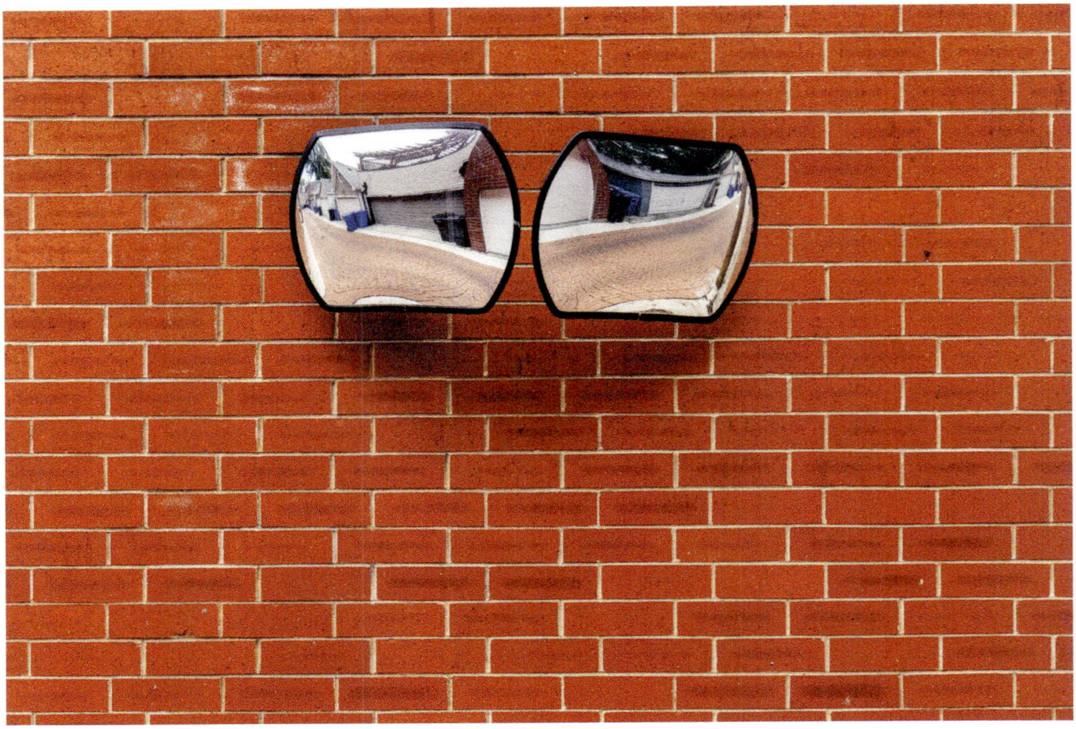

Service alley wall with mirrors in the Lincoln Park neighborhood. September 2023.

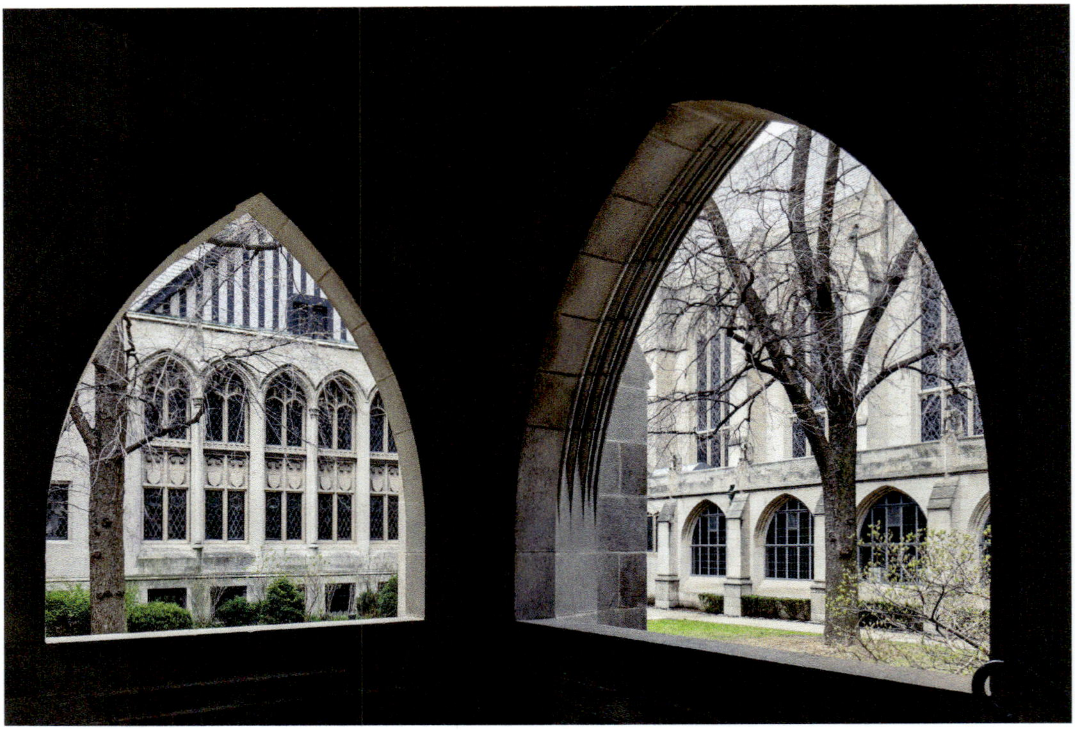

Courtyard of the Fourth Presbyterian Church on Michigan Avenue. April 2025.

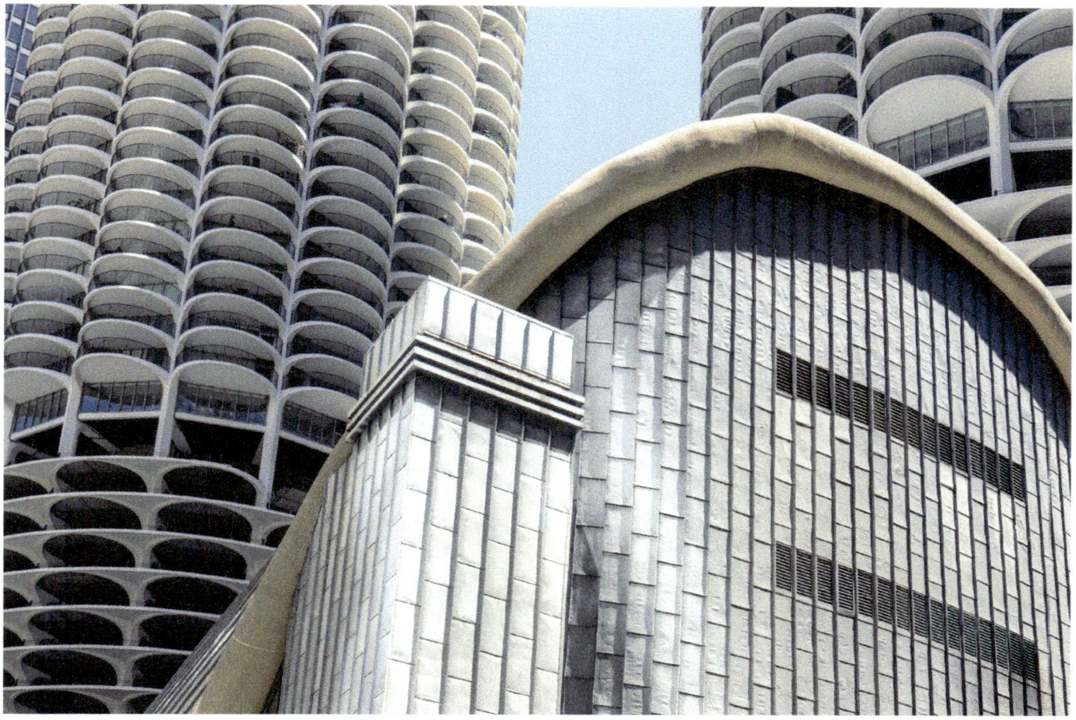

House of Blues. June 2022.

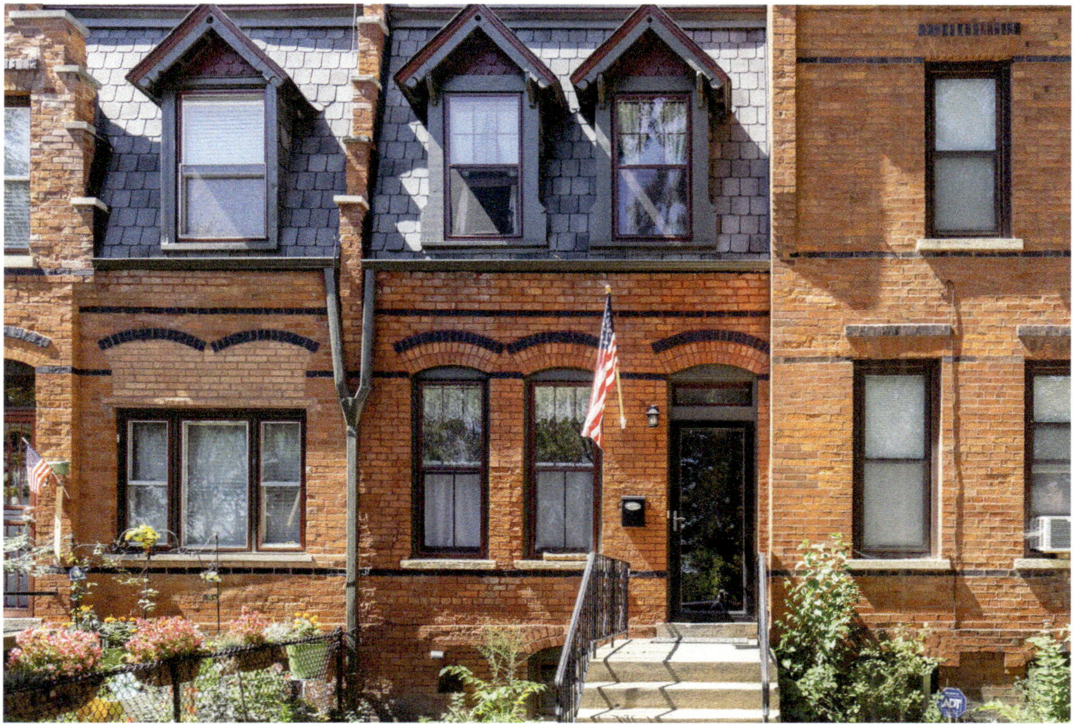

Worker's houses in the Pullman National Historic Park. September 2021.

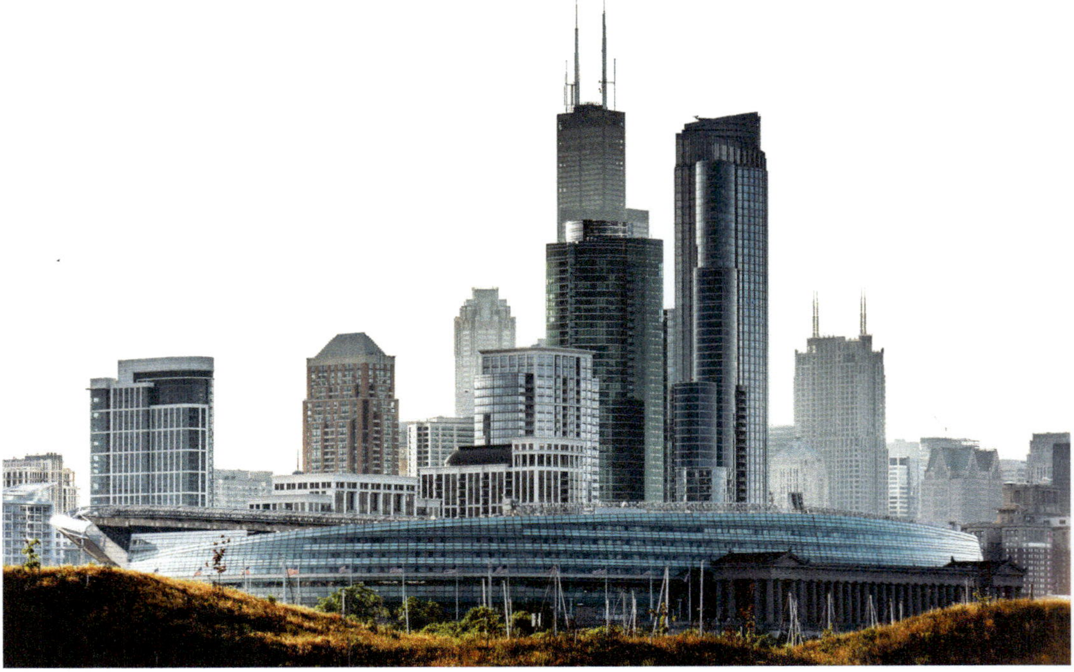

Soldier Field and the Loop viewed from Northerly Island. The tallest skyscrapers are One Museum Park and the Willis Tower. July 2016.

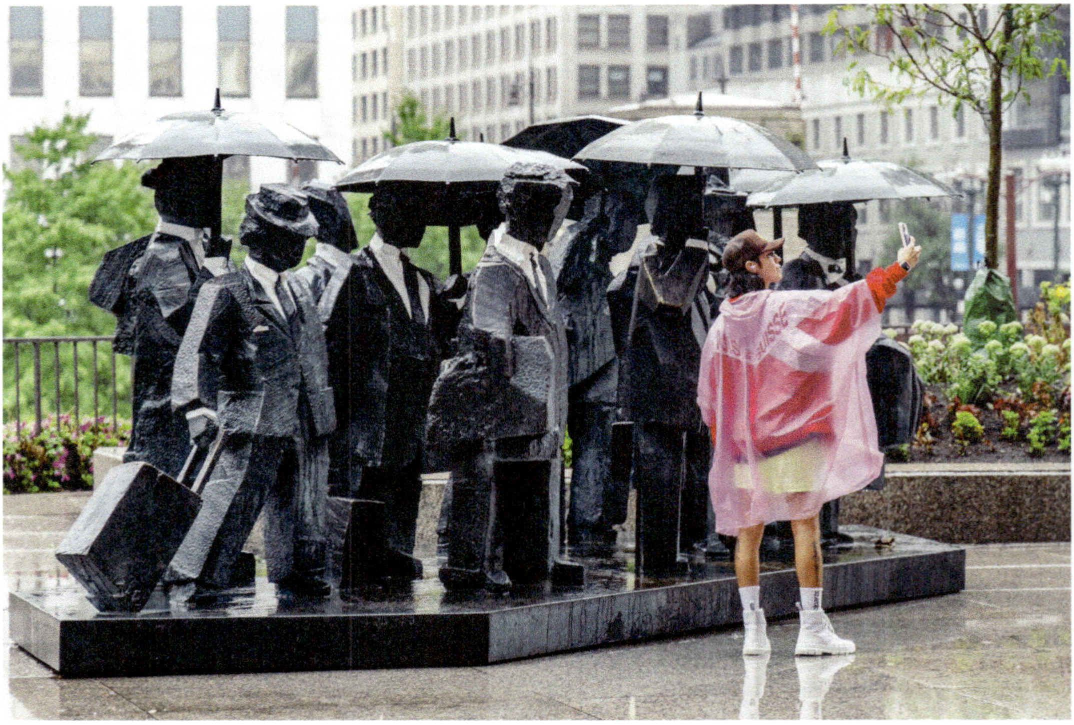

Tiny Happy Man's Statues in The Langham Plaza. August 2022.

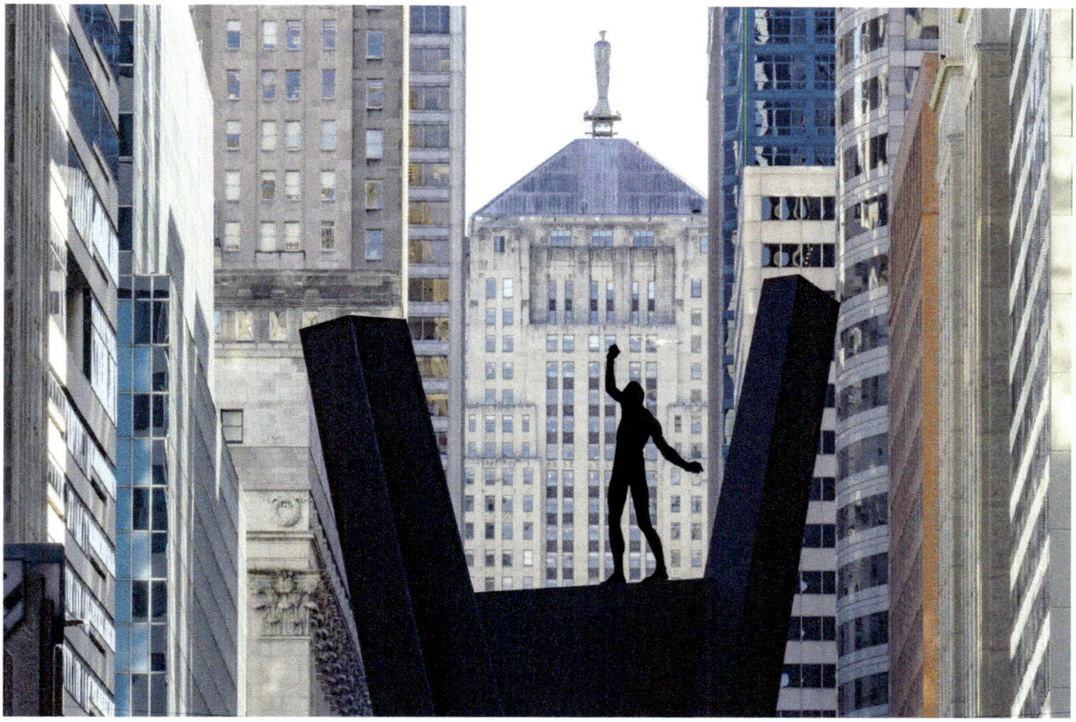

"Crossing." A sculpture by Hubertus Von Der Goltz on LaSalle Street. March 2024.

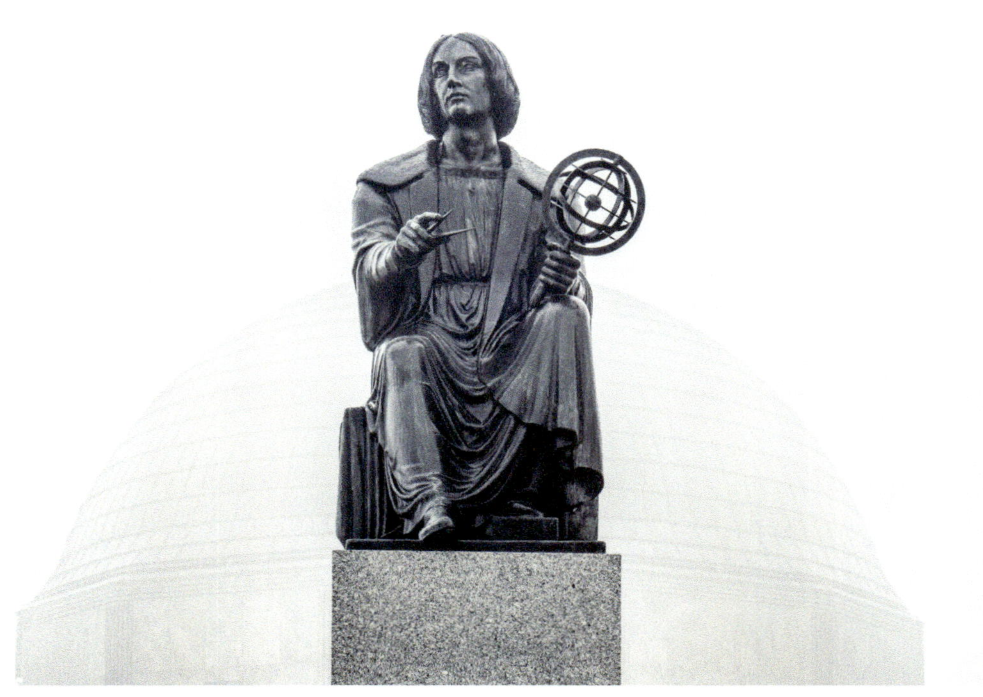

Nicolaus Copernicus Monument in front of the Adler Planetarium on the Museum Campus. December 2024.

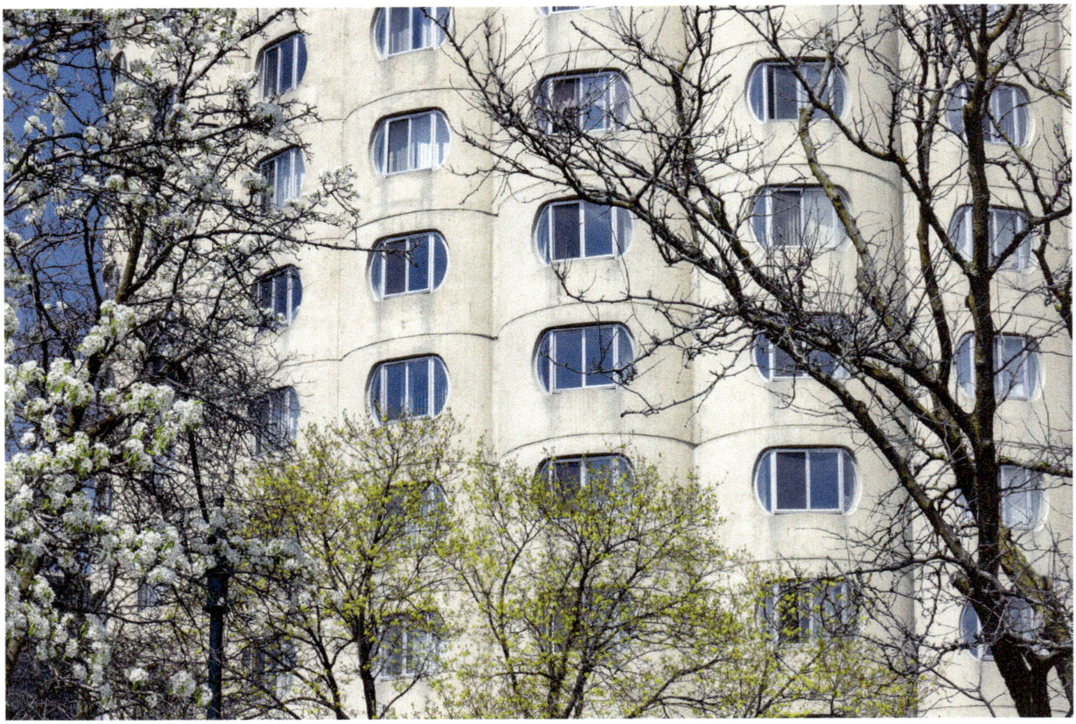

Hilliard Homes near Chinatown. April 2024.

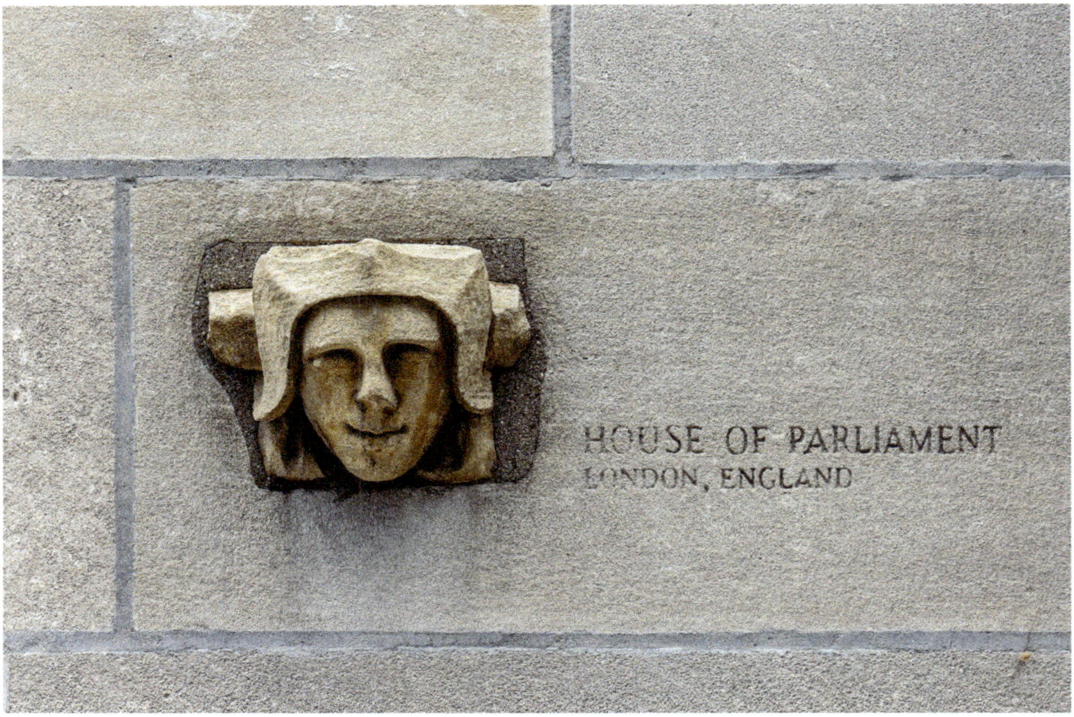

Fragment from the London Houses of Parliament embedded in the walls of the Tribune Tower. May 2025.

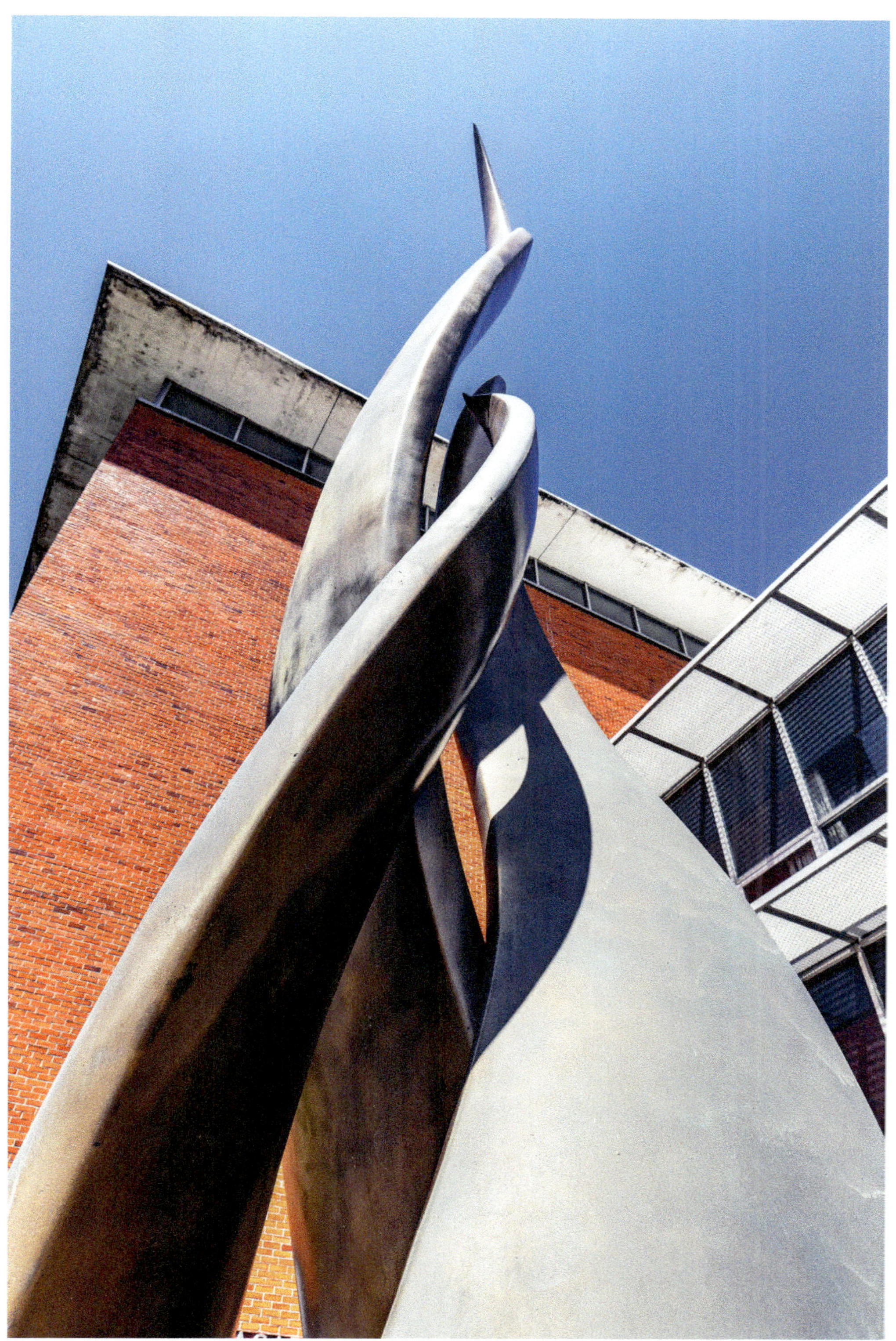

"Pillar of Fire." Chicago Fire Monument at the Chicago Fire Academy. May 2025.

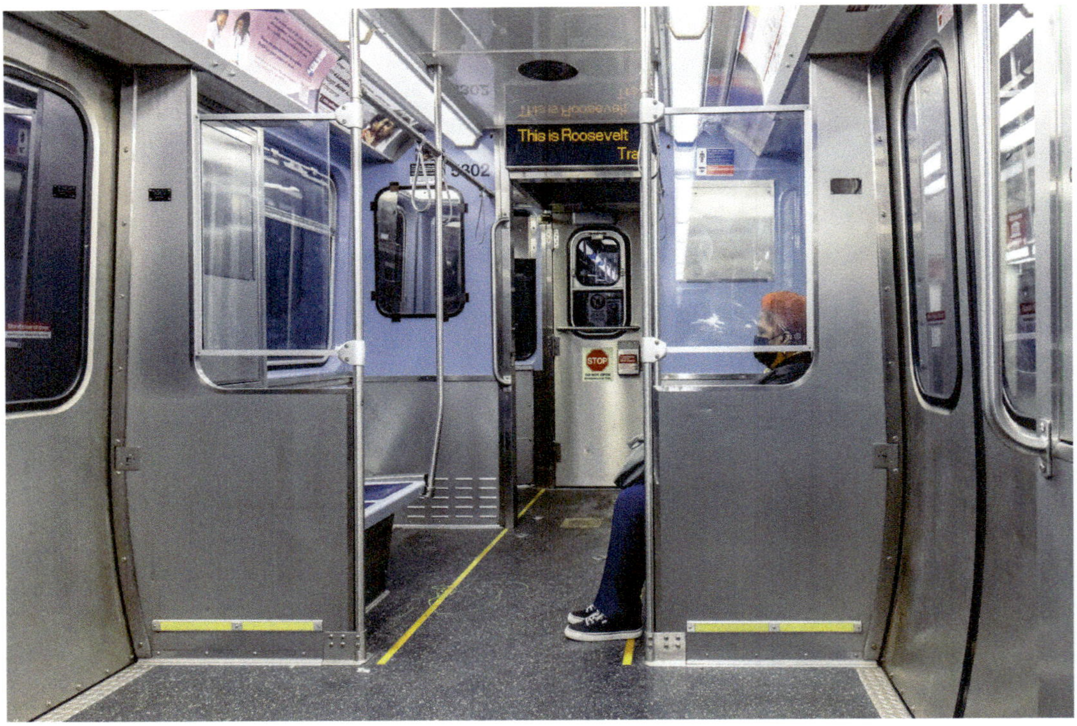

Inside a Red Line train. April 2025.

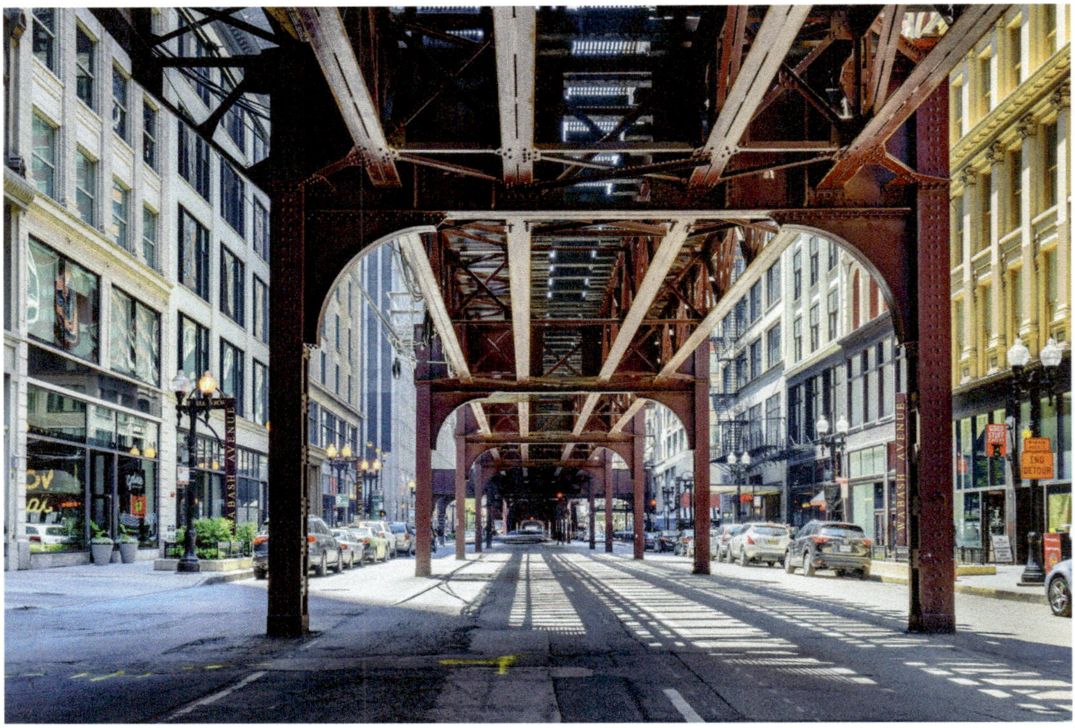

Under the L along Wabash Avenue in the Loop. June 2015.

6
The L

If you are walking in the Loop, the elevated railway (the "L") is hard to miss. Its lattice of rust red supports elevates it above Wabash Avenue as it goes due north. Becoming mustard yellow, it turns abruptly to the west at Lake Street and then south at Wells Street, before turning east at Van Buren Street to finally close the loop at Wabash Avenue. Its metalwork, which vibrates with the rattle of passing trains, creates a tunnel-like structure over the roads below. Whether you think the L in the Loop is an eyesore or a marvel, it certainly gives the neighborhood a distinct character. Outside of the Loop, the L has an extensive transportation network which is mostly above ground. In 2024, the L had 224 miles of track and 146 stations with 1,480 rail cars in operation. The oldest L structure is the Garfield station house on the Green Line. It was built the year the L began operations in 1892, as part of the railway system connecting downtown Chicago with the 1893 World's Columbian Exposition. In modern times the L provides a convenient and relatively rapid way to get around the Loop and far beyond with twenty-four-hour service on the Red and Blue lines. It is easy to use. You can pay by tapping in with a credit card.

Photographer Tips

i) Some L stations, for example at Wabash and Adams, have pedestrian bridges over the tracks. They provide a great way to get overhead views of the trains.

ii) If you want an excuse to use the L, consider a trip to Chinatown which is on the Red Line and is just a couple of stops south of the Loop. This segment of the Red Line is, however, mostly below ground.

iii) As the Brown Line crosses the river on the Wells Street Bridge there is a good, elevated view of several Main Stem river bridges.

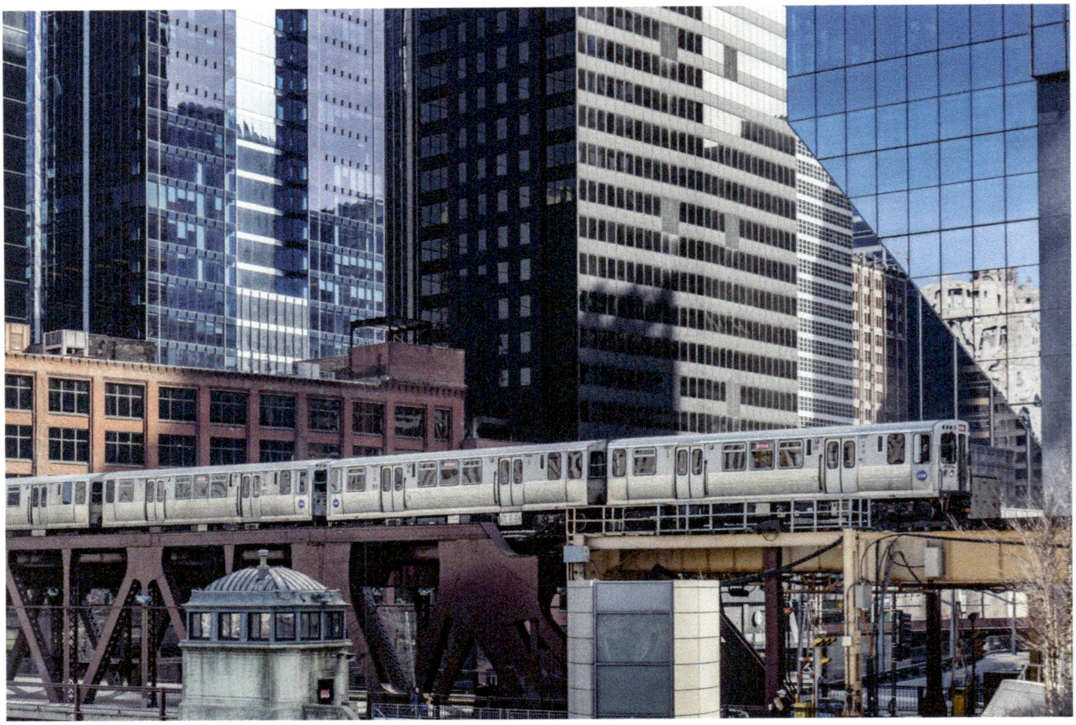

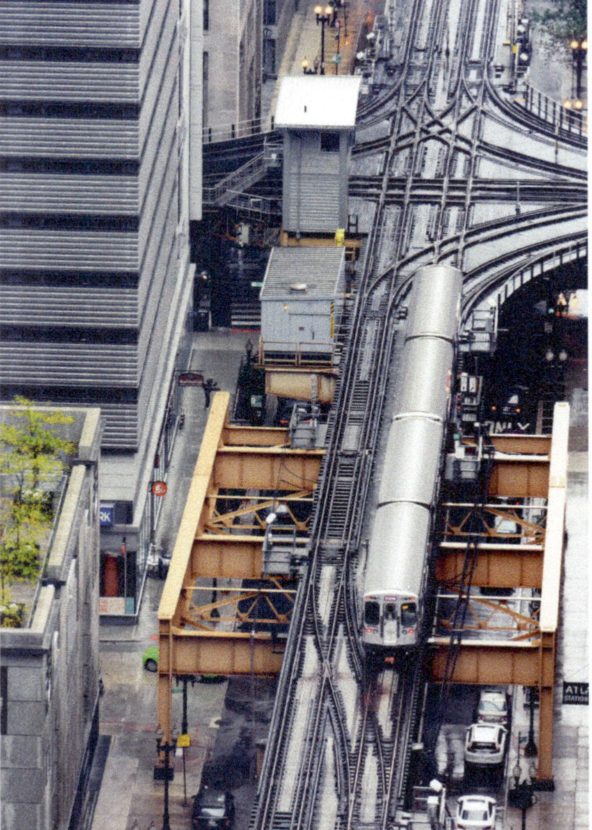

Above: The L crossing the river on the Lake Street Bridge. March 2018.

Left: The Tower 18 Junction at Lake and Wells Streets. October 2017.

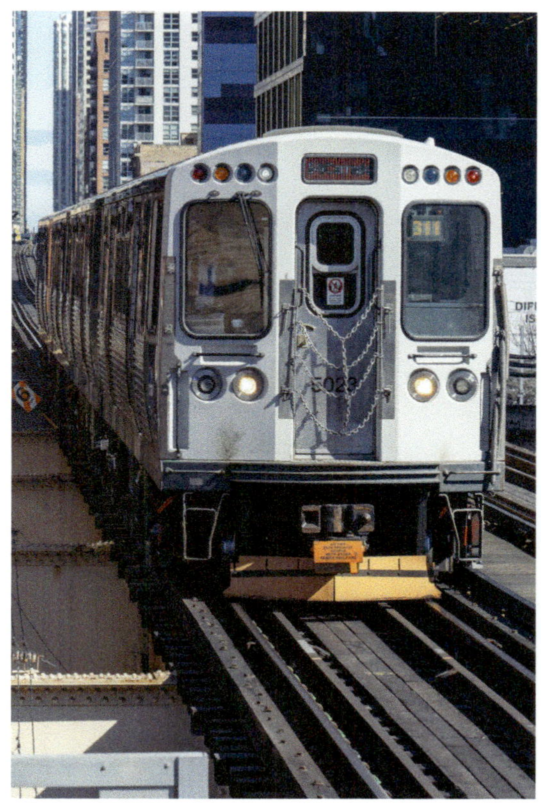

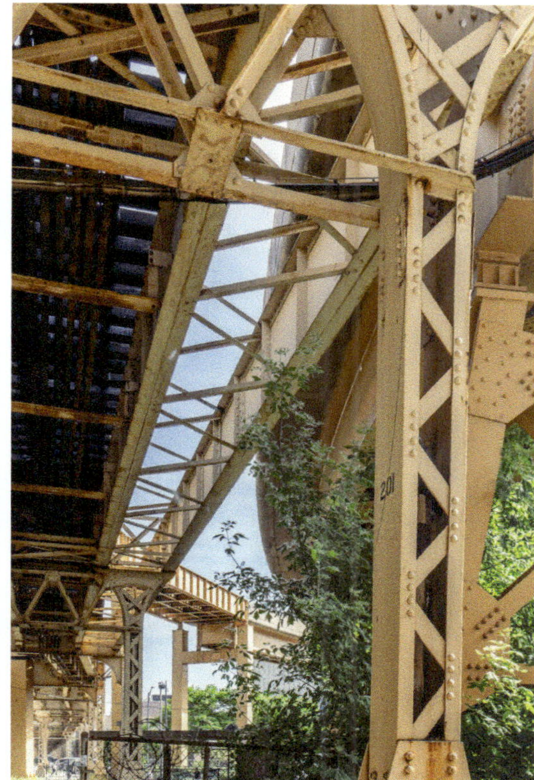

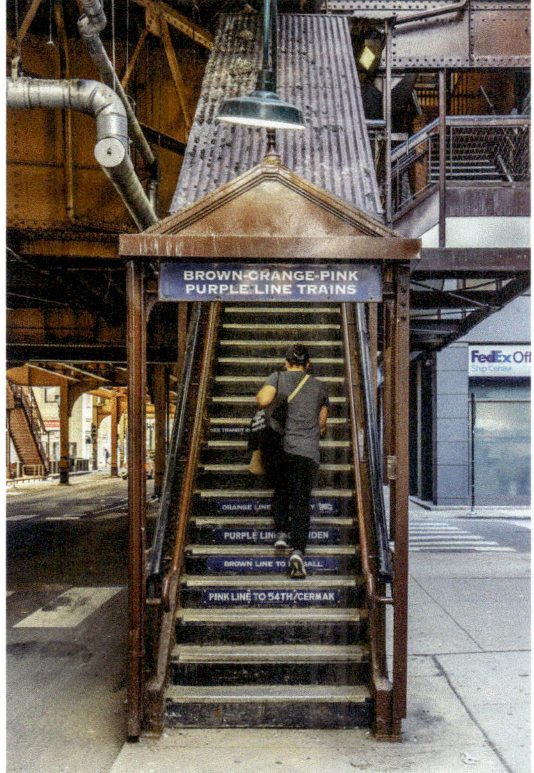

Above left: Orange Line train on the L at Lake Street. March 2024.

Above right: Red and Green Line split at 18th Street. June 2023.

Right: Entrance to Quincy Station in the Loop. April 2023.

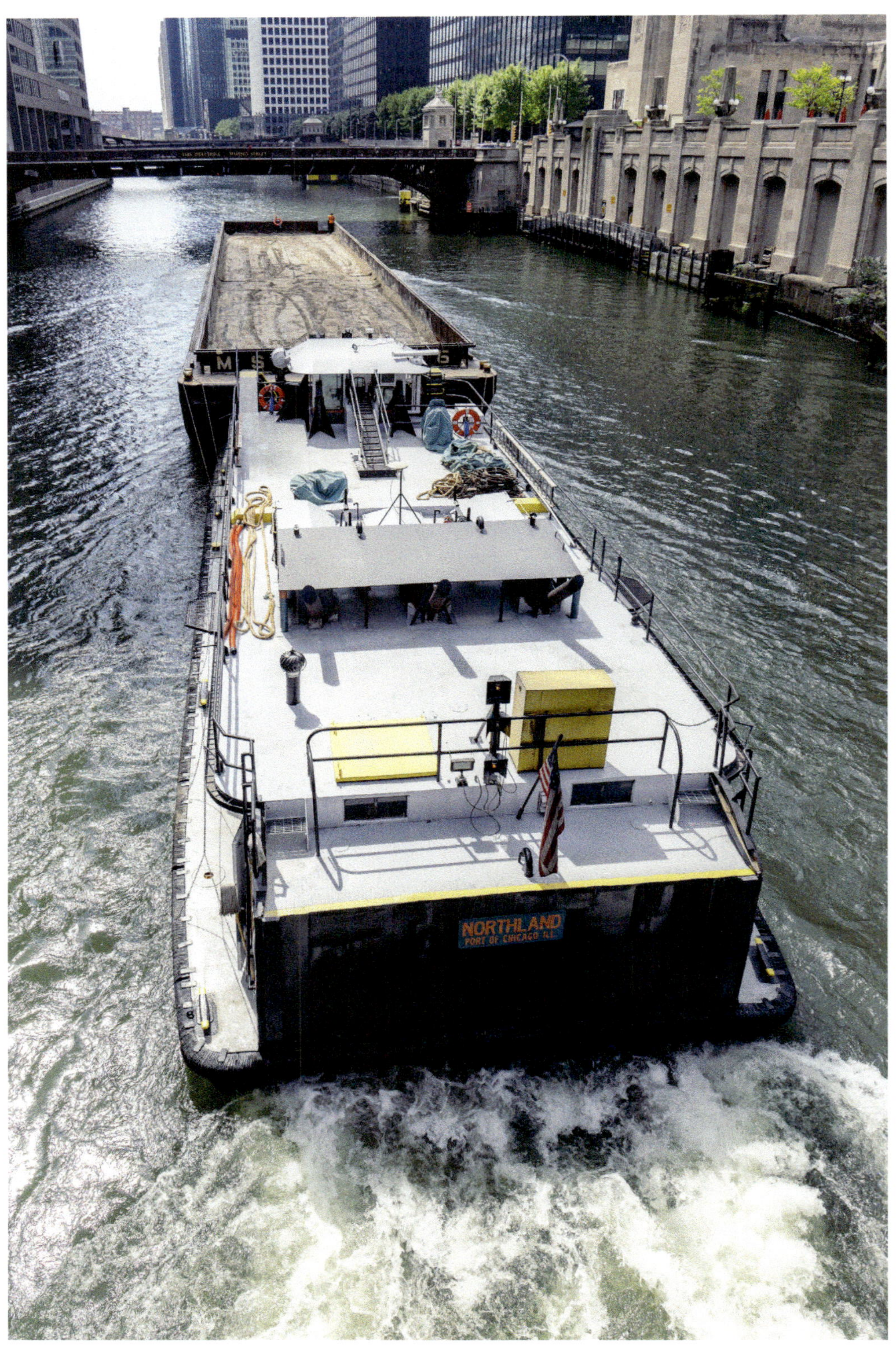

River Barge on the South Branch of the Chicago River. September 2022.

7
Industry

In 1914 Carl Sandburg published his "Chicago" poem which begins with the lines: "Hog Butcher for the World, Tool Maker, Stacker of Wheat, Player with Railroads and the Nation's Freight Handler, Stormy, husky, brawling … " Much of the industry that inspired those words can no longer be found in Chicago. The grain silos, stockyards, and steel mills have gone, but Chicago remains a rail transportation and distribution hub and there are other industries beyond the downtown area. In spirit, Sandburg's lines still ring true. Construction is perhaps the most visible of the heavier industries remaining in the city center. At the time of writing, the Thompson Center is being remodeled, a skyscraper is under construction at 400 Lake Shore, and the Chicago Tribune Freedom Center is being demolished to make way for a riverside casino. All this construction requires lots of concrete which is supplied by several concrete plants not far from downtown. River barges can sometimes be seen on the North and South Branches transporting the required bulk materials. Other major commercial downtown activities include finance, retail, and tourism. This non-manufacturing sector of the economy is still recovering from the 2020–2023 pandemic which closed one in three stores along State Street in the Loop. However, the shopping streets are vibrant and in 2023 Chicago welcomed 52 million visitors.

Photographer Tips

i) The steel mills are not far from Chicago. On clear days, with binoculars or a telephoto lens, smokestacks in Indiana can be seen across the lake.
ii) During the annual "Open House Chicago" weekend in October, several industrial sites are open to visitors. A site list is available online a few weeks before the event.

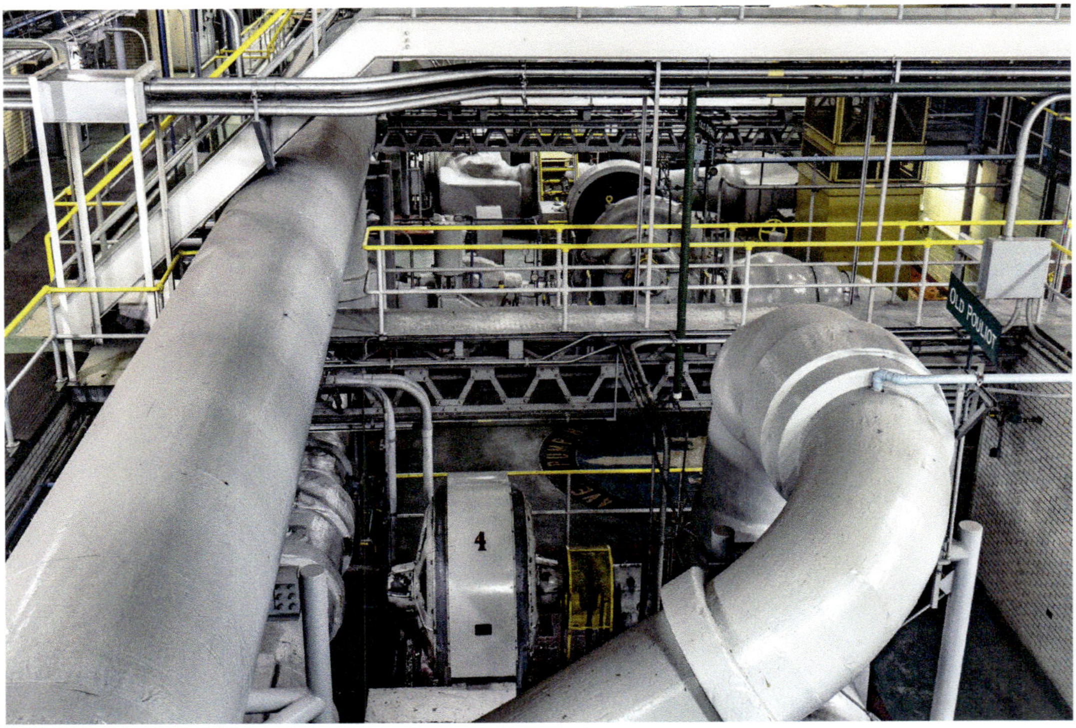

Inside the Chicago Avenue Pumping Station. April 2025.

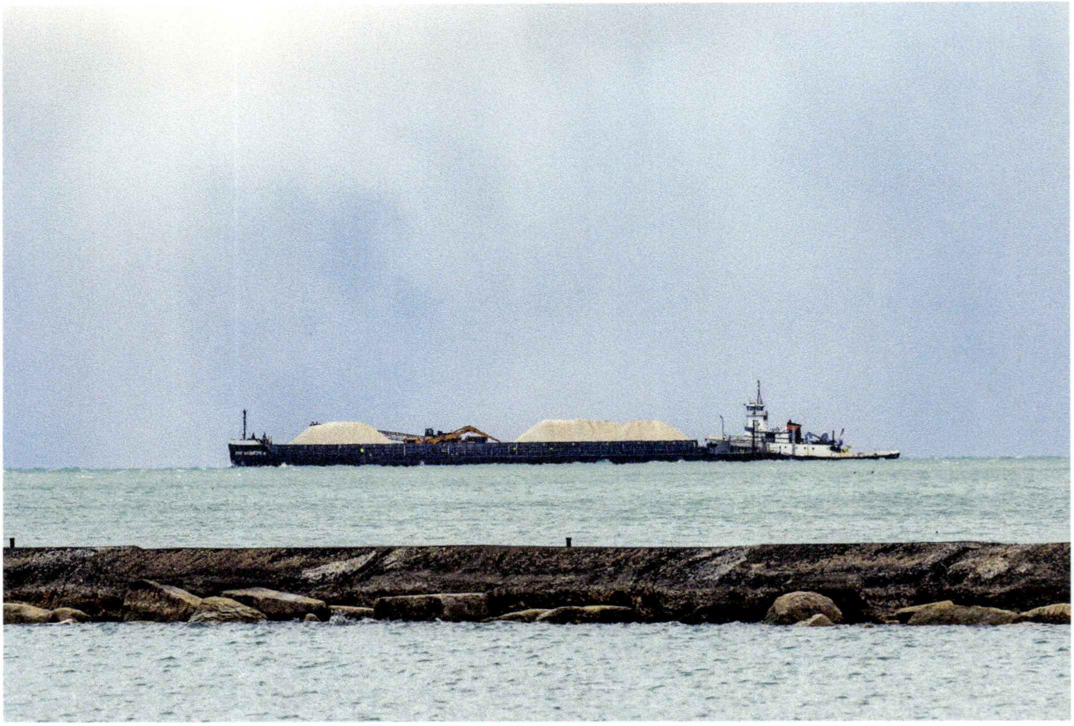

Industrial barge on Lake Michigan viewed from Monroe Harbor. January 2025.

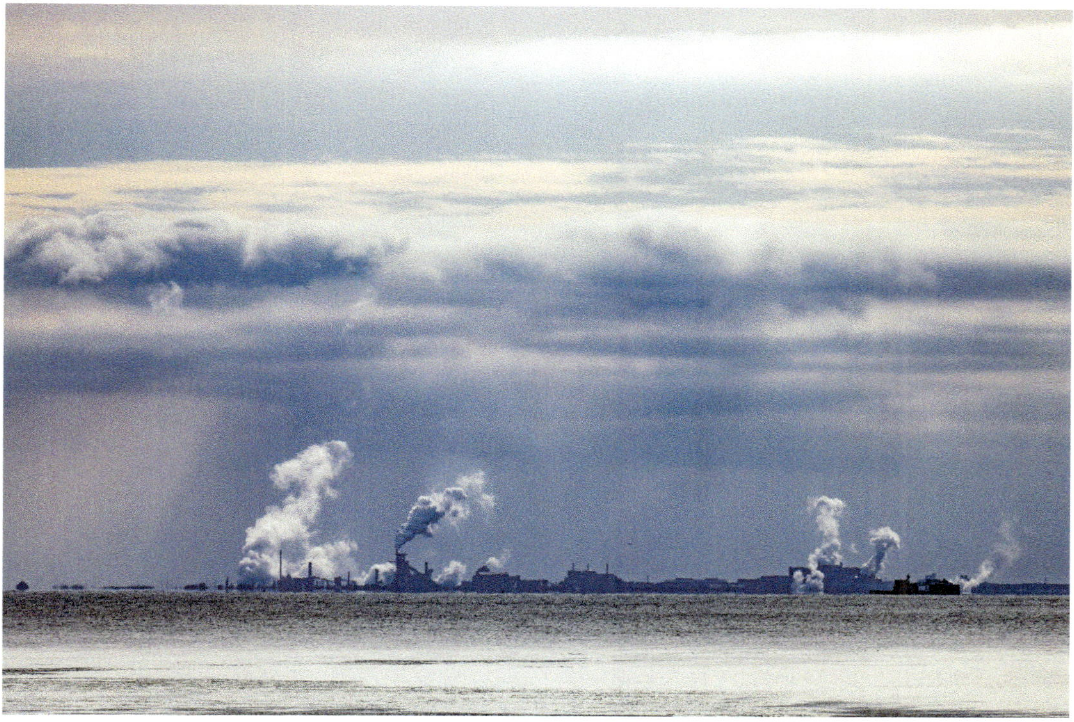

Industry in Indiana across Lake Michigan, viewed from the Loop. February 2025.

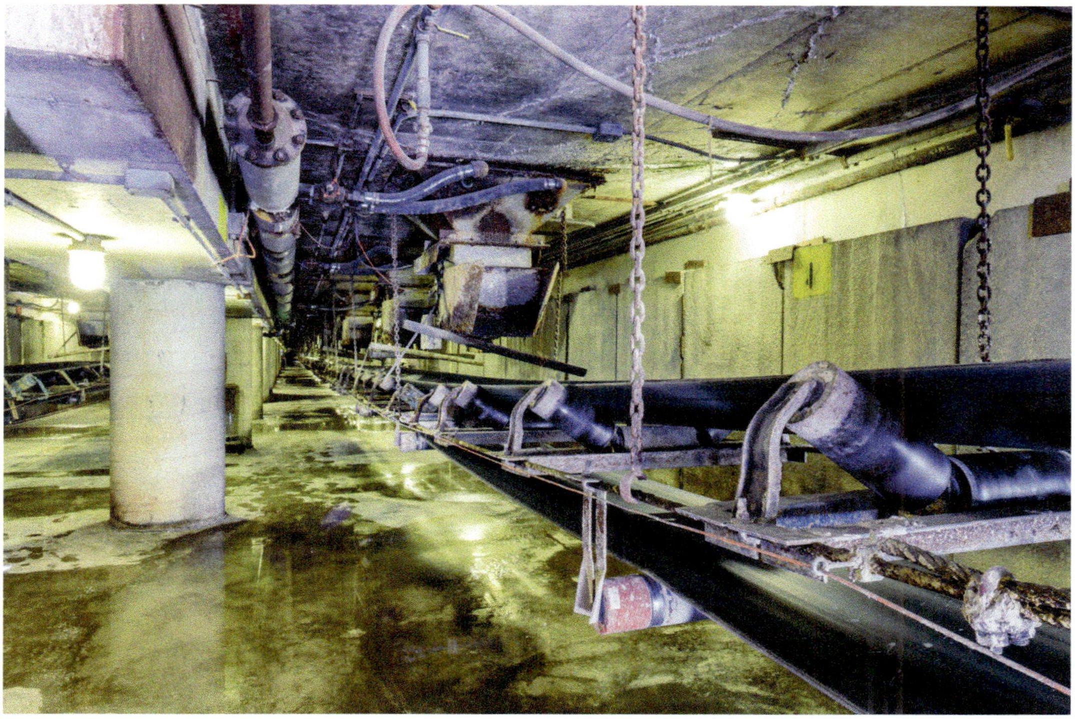

Inside a concrete mixing plant in the West Town neighborhood. October 2015.

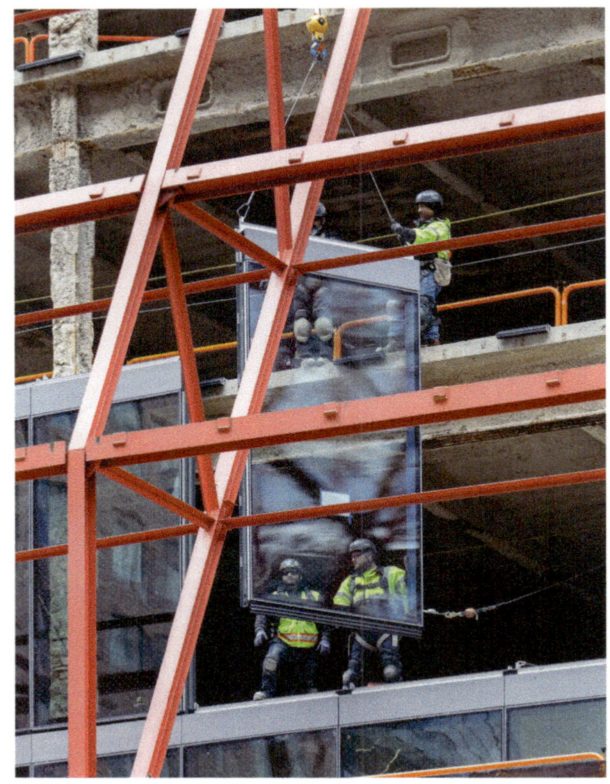

Redevelopment of the Thompson Center.
March 2025.

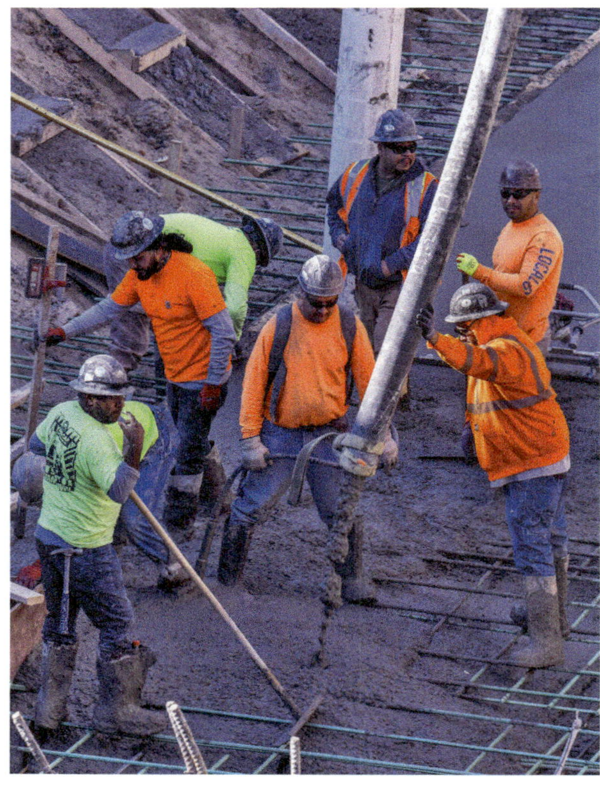

Pouring concrete for the construction of
400 Lake Shore. December 2024.

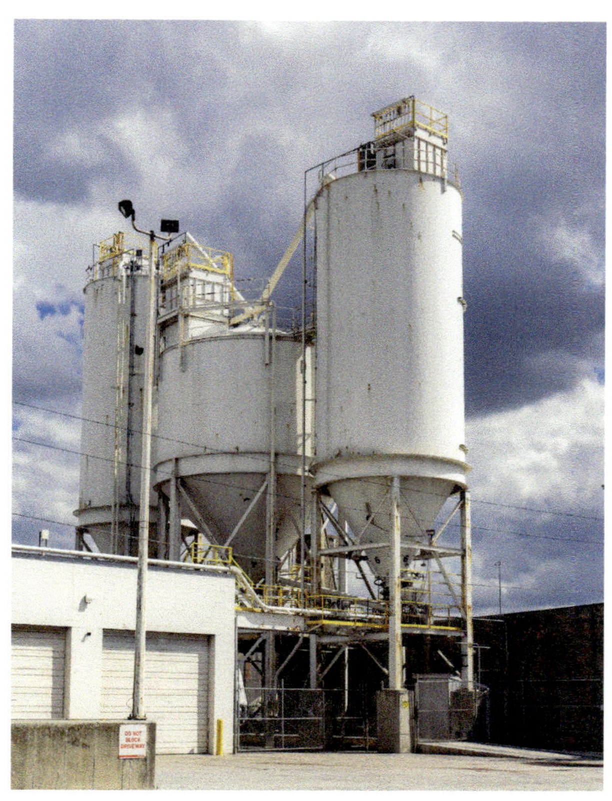

Ozinga concrete mixing plant. May 2024.

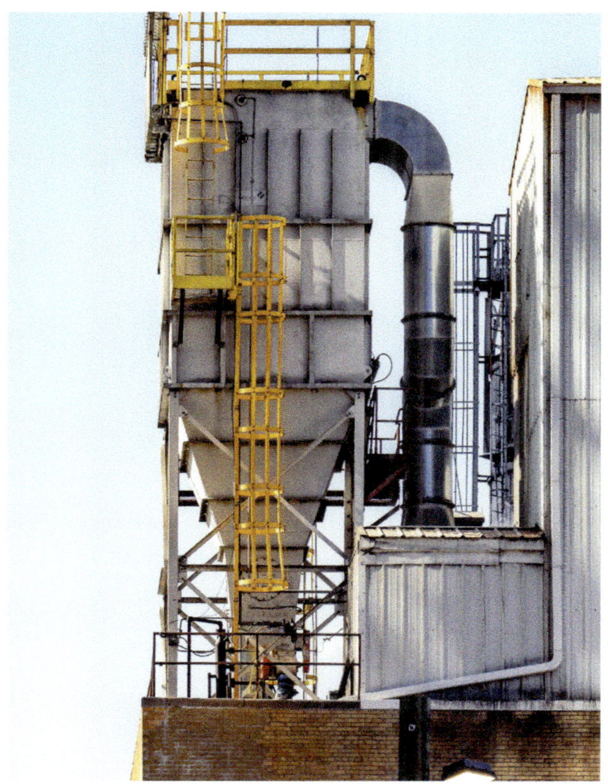

Blommer Chocolate Company. March 2024.

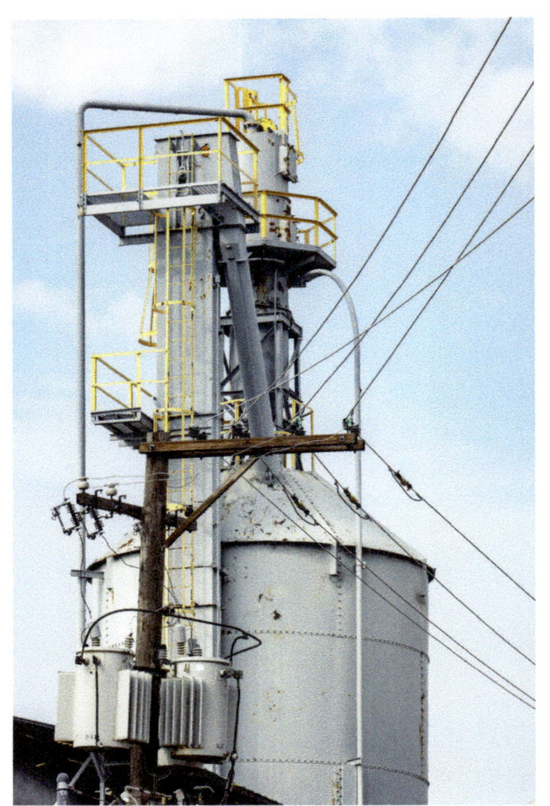

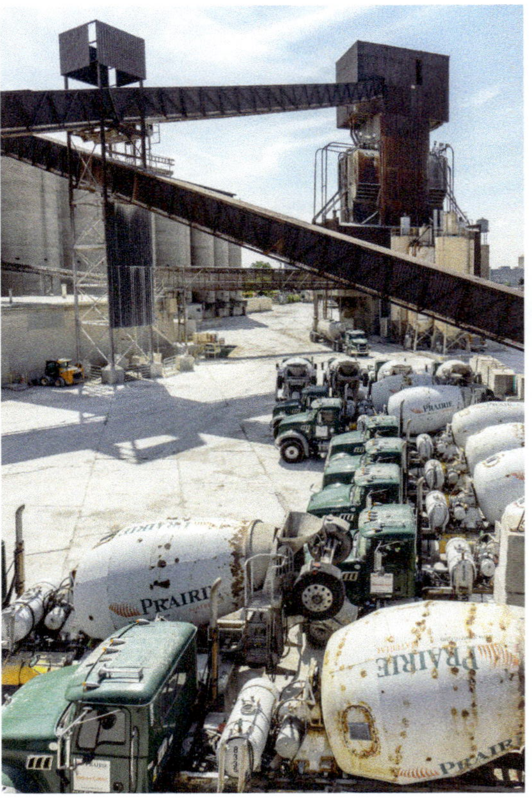

Above left: Sipi Metals. October 2024.

Above right: Prairie Materials concrete mixing plant. July 2022.

Left: Railyard viewed from 18th Street West Pedestrian Bridge. April 2025.

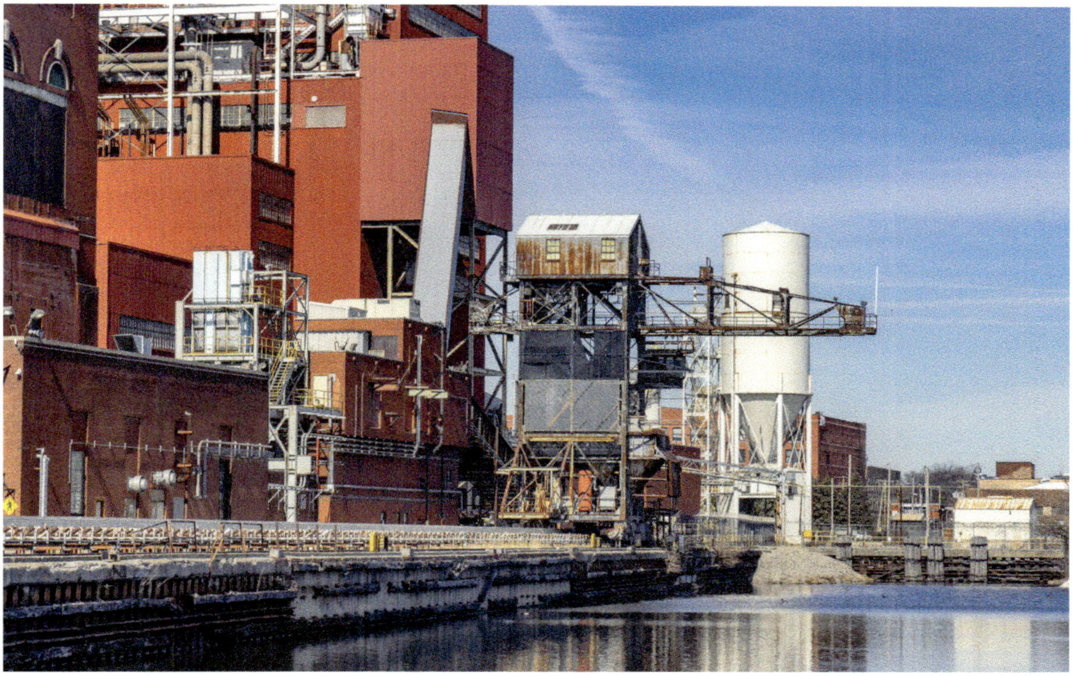

Fisk Generating Station (closed in 2012) on the South Branch of the Chicago River. March 2025.

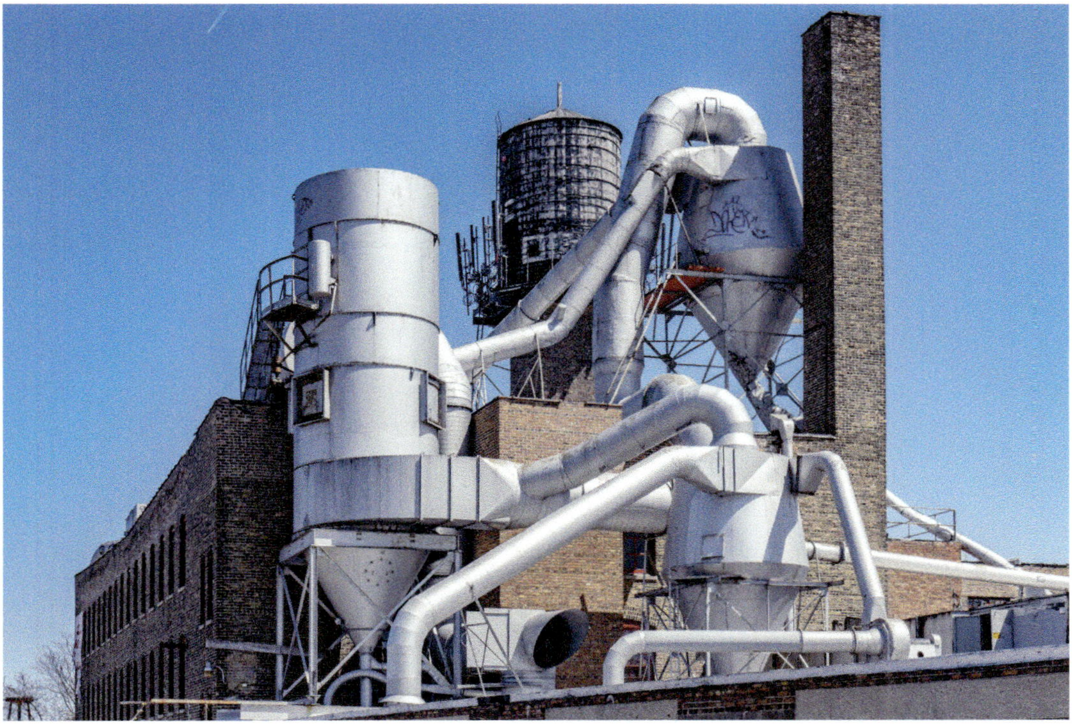

Former Lincoln Logs Toy factory in the Humboldt Park neighborhood. April 2018.

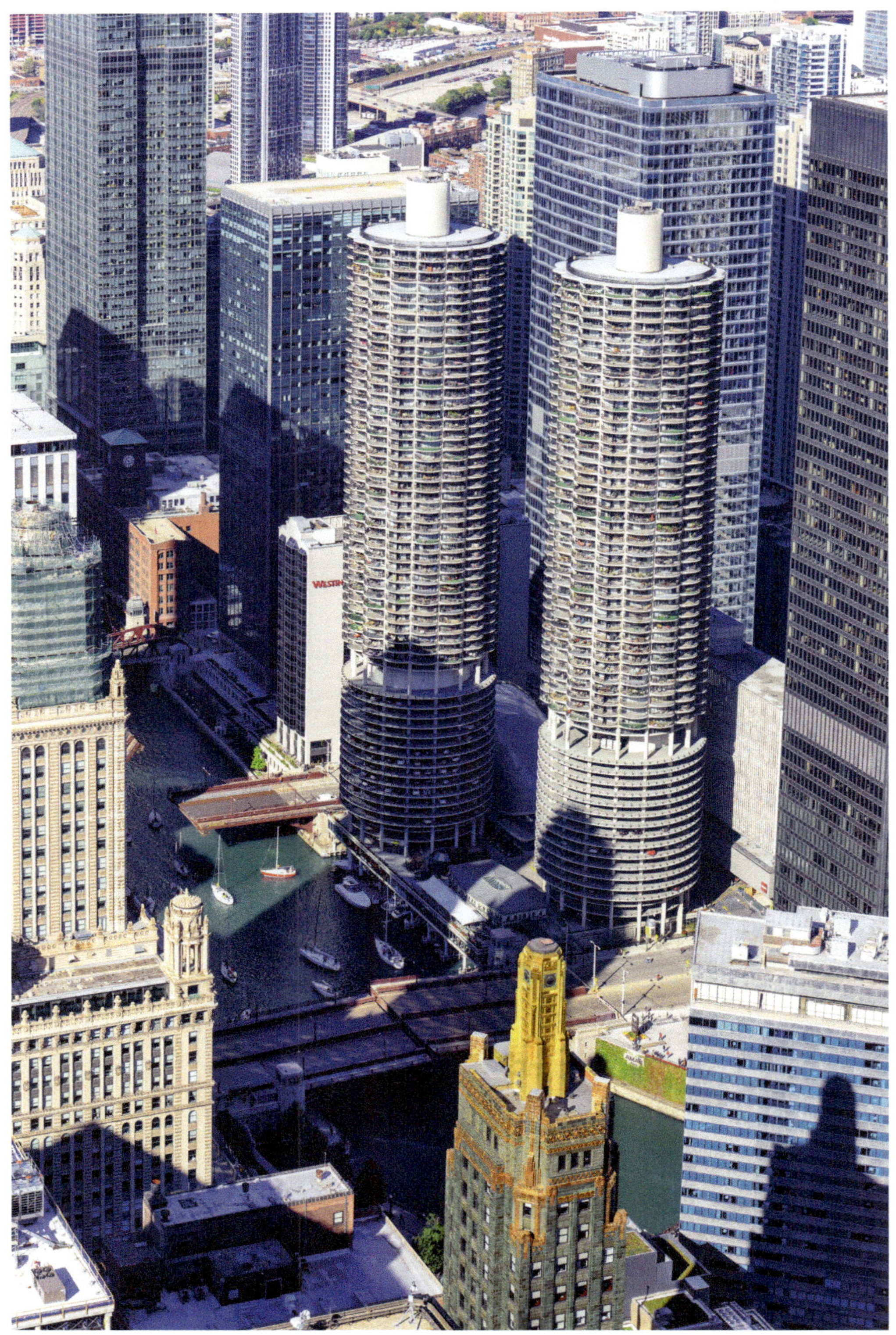

Skyscrapers by the Chicago River. Marina City Towers in the center. October 2015.

8
Go High

Chicago is a city of skyscrapers, which means it's possible to go high and get a bird's-eye perspective. If you want to use a drone, it must be kept below 400 feet and there are restrictions on where you can fly. Flying drones in Chicago parks, for example, is prohibited. There are a couple of iconic buildings in Chicago with public viewing spaces well above 400 feet. The Willis Tower in the Loop has a Skydeck 1,353 feet above street level. North of the river, 875 North Michigan Avenue has a 1,030-foot-high observation deck. Other opportunities to go high include bars and restaurants with excellent views and several high-rise parking structures with views over the L. A couple of years ago I noticed what appeared to be a public space on the top of a hotel skyscraper that overlooked the river. To investigate, I entered the building and took the elevator to the top. The space turned out to be a large empty event room with 360-degree views. I was not sure I was supposed to be there, but there was nothing to stop me from entering and taking photographs. After a little while a janitor appeared at the door and looked at me. He came over and I thought I was in trouble. Instead, he said, "Do you want to go on the roof?" We walked through a cobwebbed room with elevator machinery and then climbed out onto the roof. There were spectacular views of the river from the top of a 39-story skyscraper. Sometimes it pays to be bold!

Photographer Tips

i) When photographing through windows, place the lens against the glass to minimize reflections.

ii) Consider using a long-focal-length lens when going high. This will give you more opportunities to make images beyond the normal.

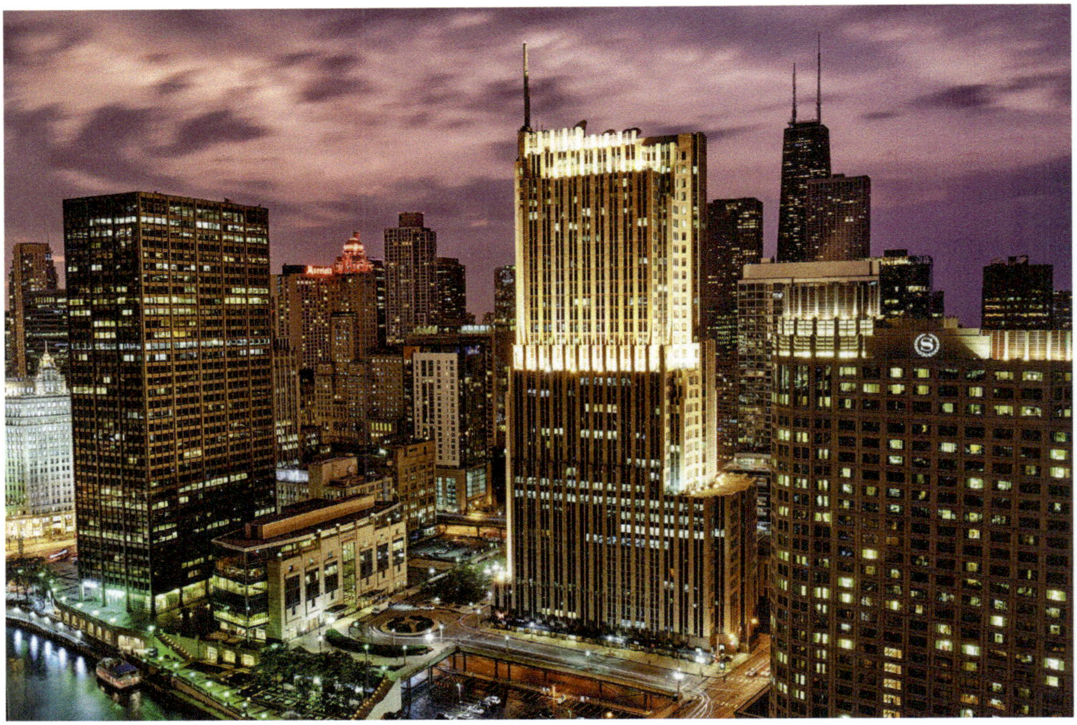

Skyscrapers at dusk. Equitable Building (left) and NBC Tower (center). June 2015.

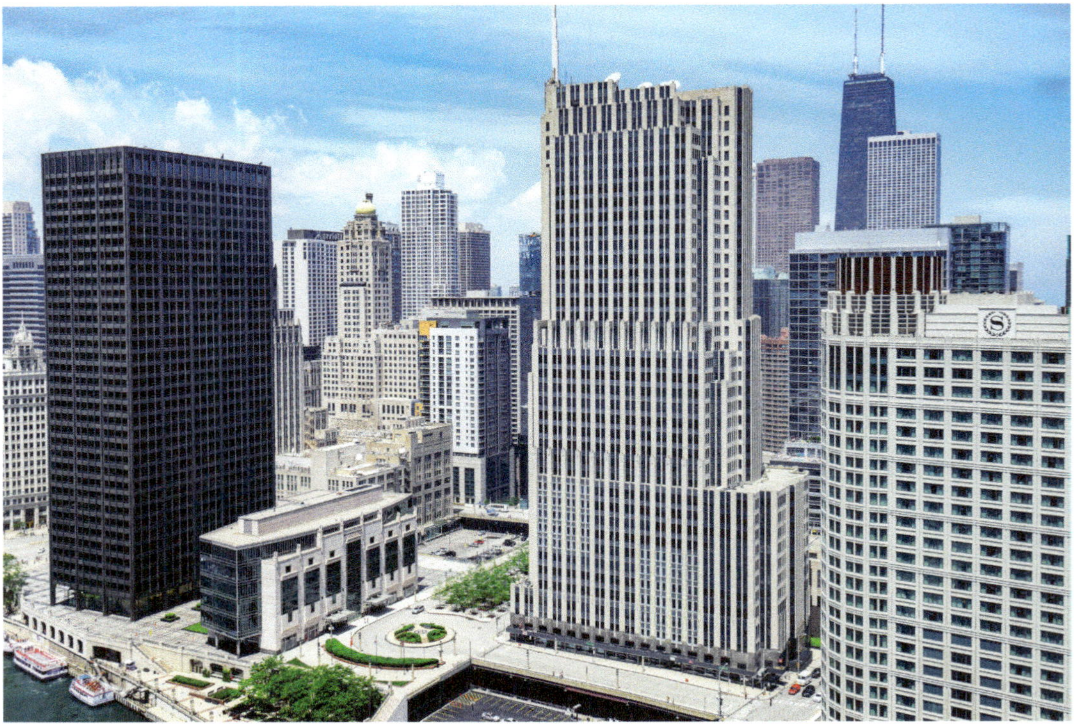

Equitable Building and Gleacher Center (left), NBC Tower (right of center). June 2015.

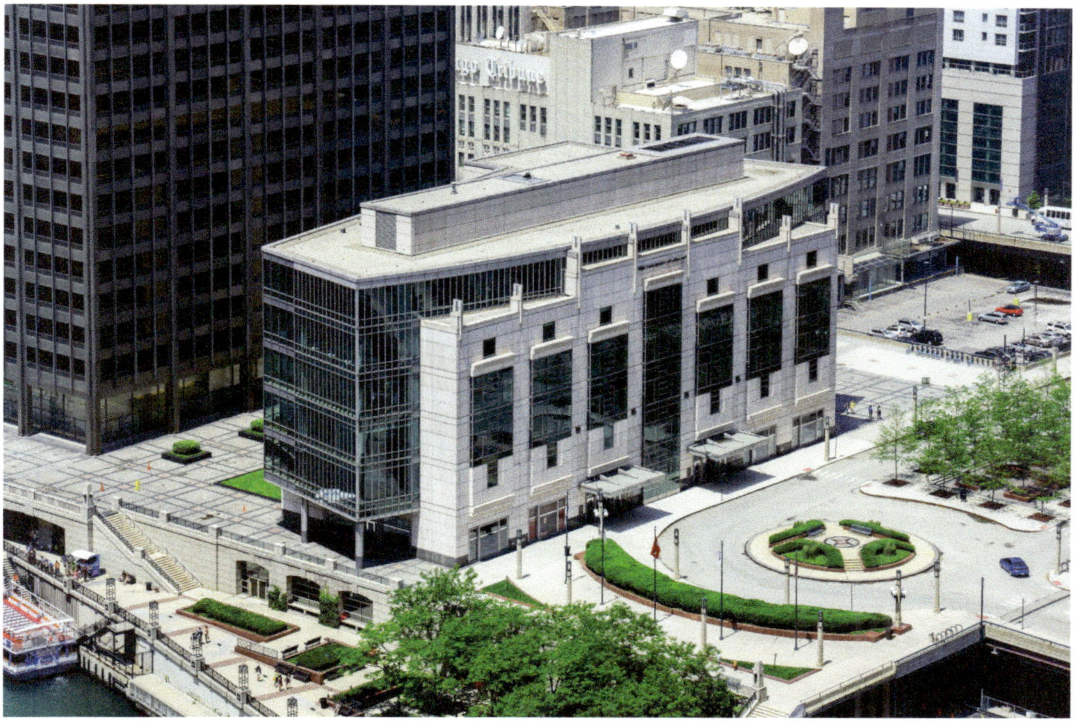

The Gleacher Center in Streeterville. June 2015.

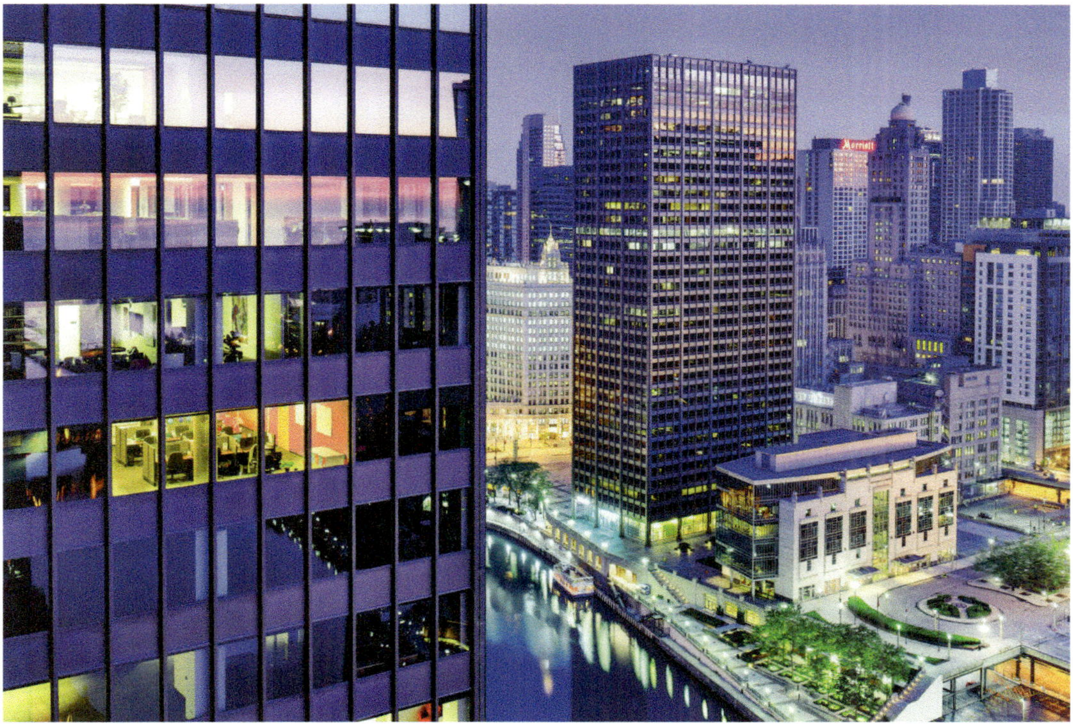

Skyscrapers at sunrise. The KPMG Building, Equitable Building and Gleacher Center beside the Chicago River. June 2015.

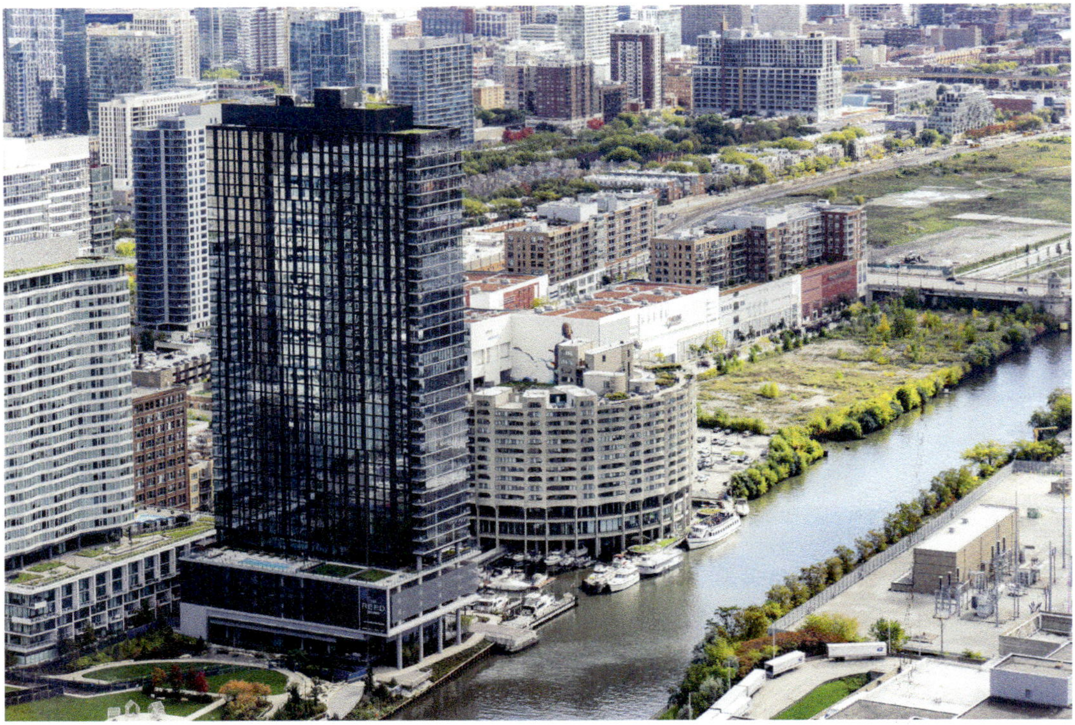

South Branch of the Chicago River. The curved building is River City. October 2023.

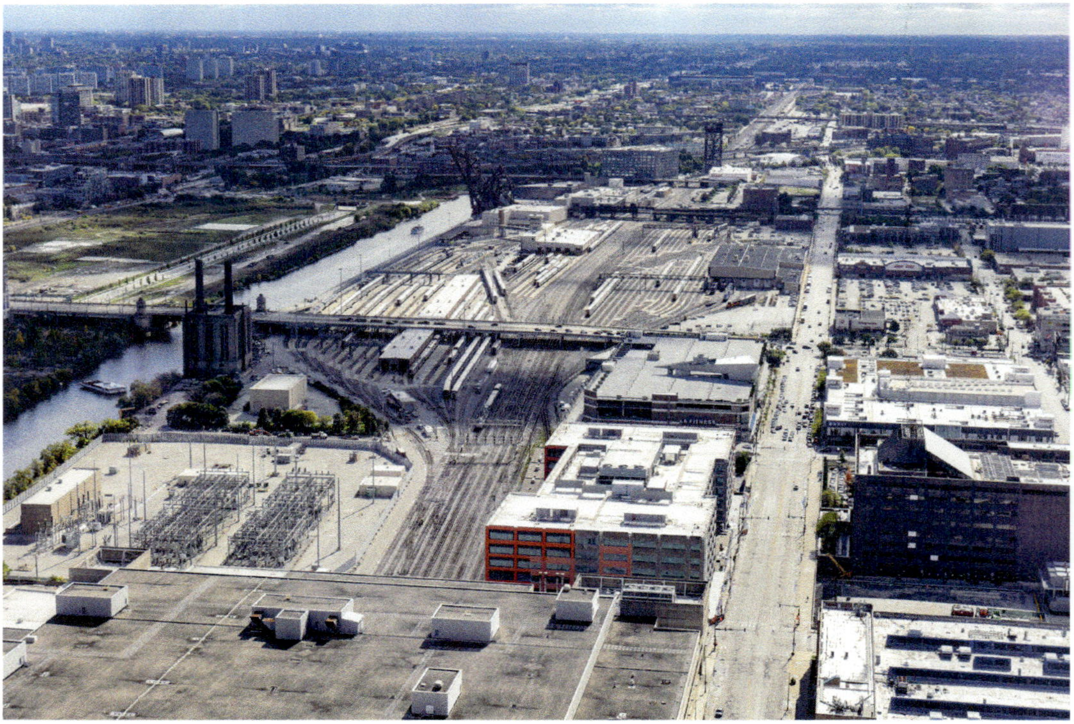

Railyards south of the Loop. October 2023.

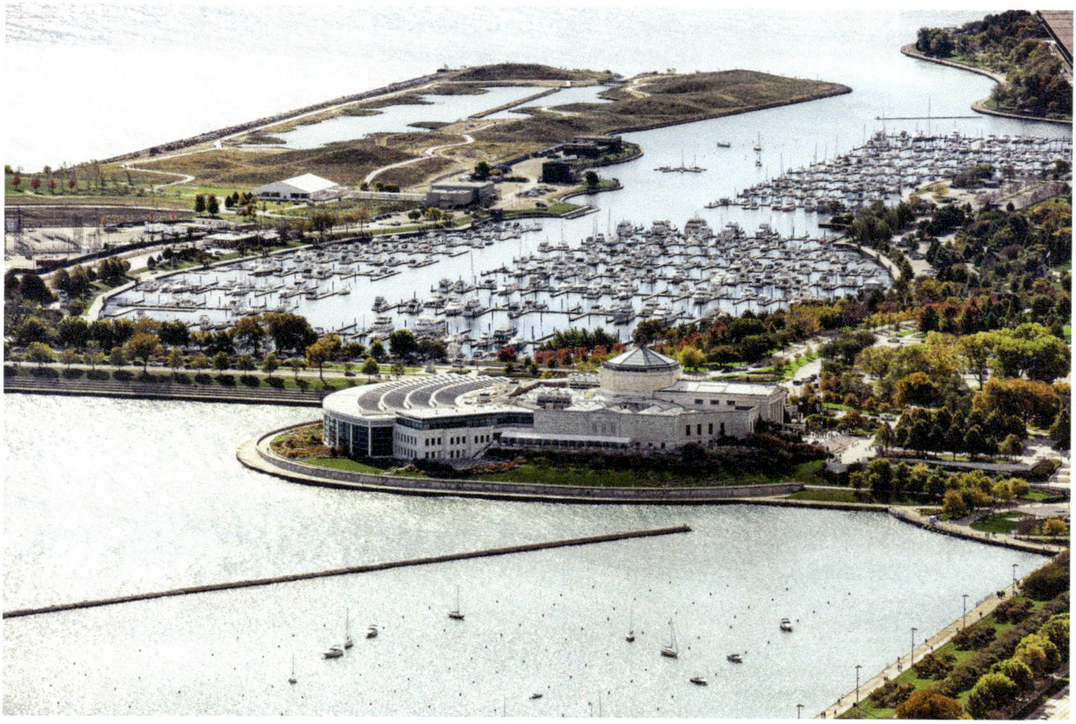

The Shedd Aquarium, Burnham Harbor and Northerly Island. October 2015.

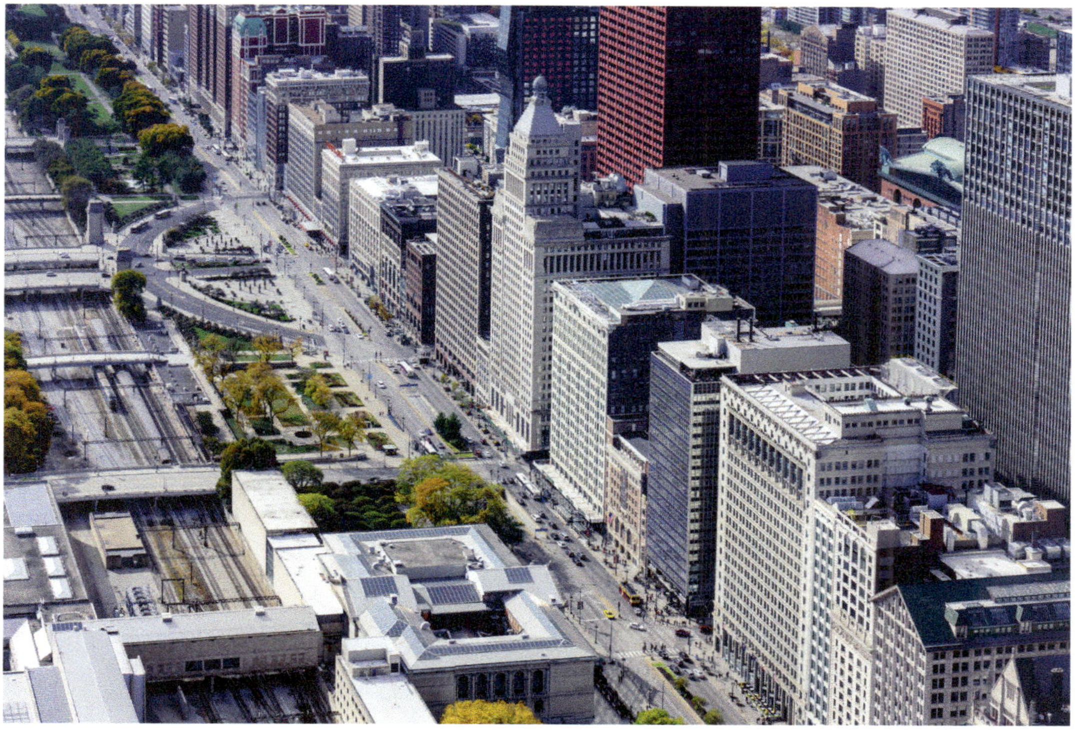

Michigan Avenue in the Loop. October 2015.

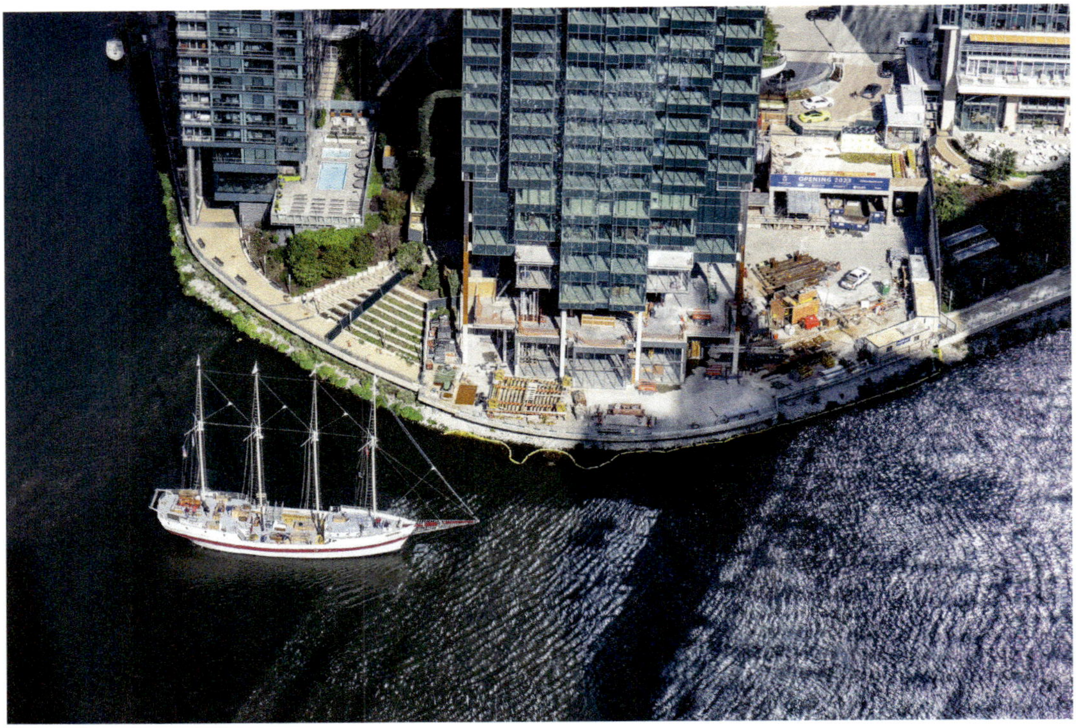

Tall ship at Wolf Point with Salesforce Tower under construction. October 2021.

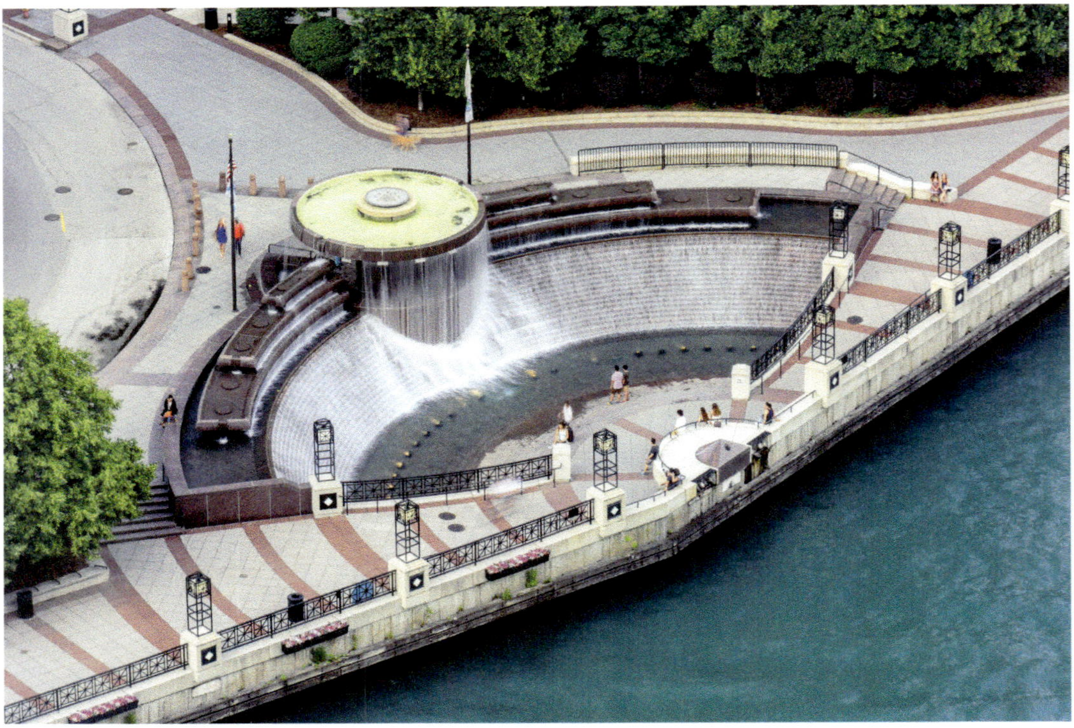

The Nicholas J. Melas Centennial Fountain on the Main Stem of the Chicago River. June 2015.

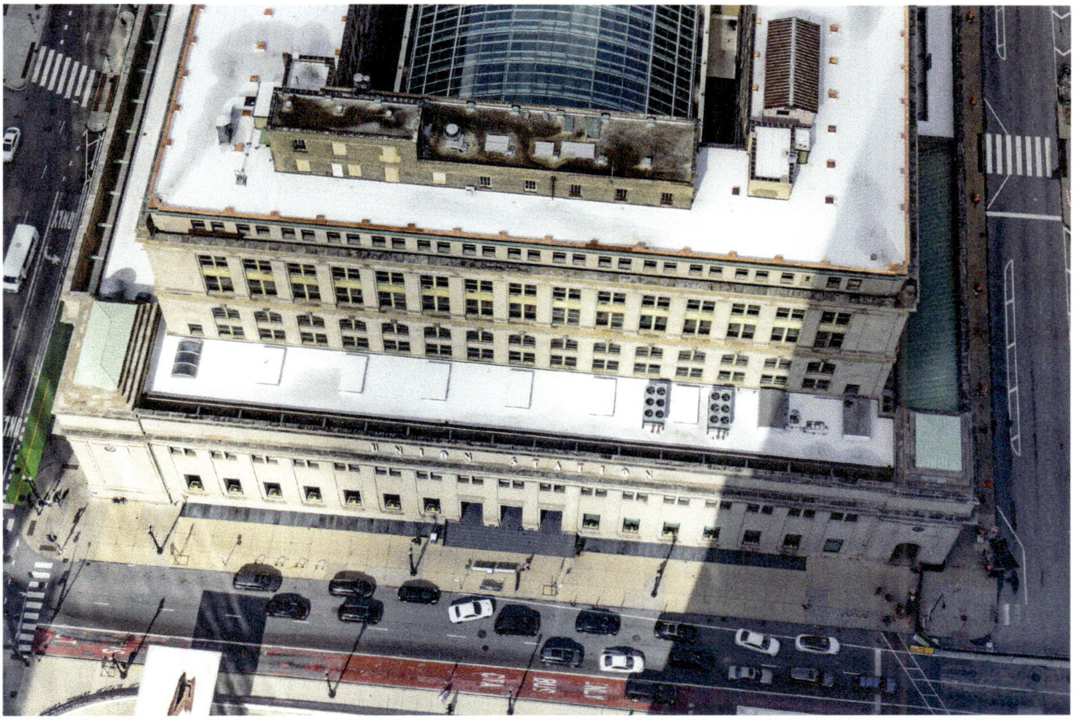

Union Station. October 2023.

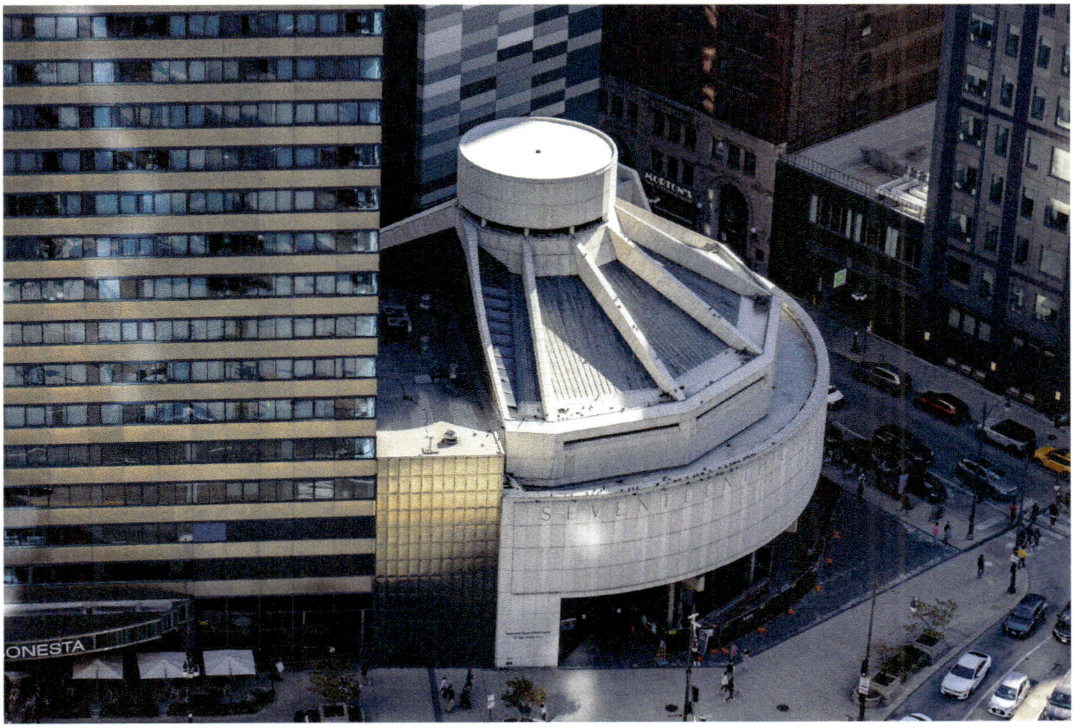

Seventeenth Church of Christ, Scientist in the Loop. October 2024.

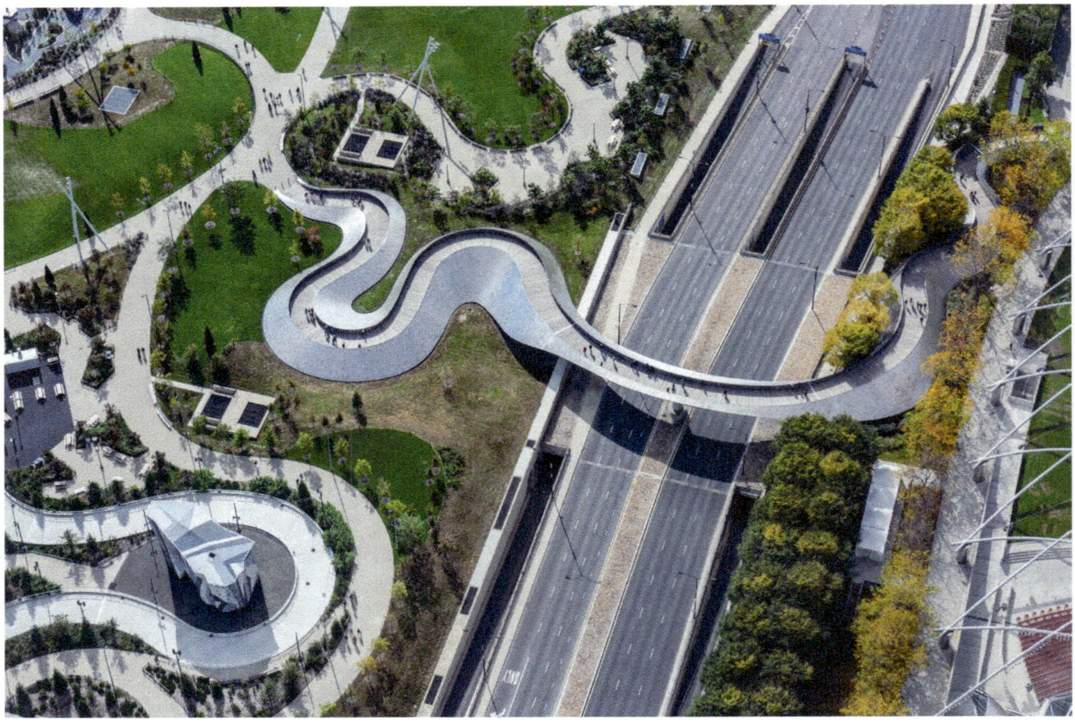

BP Pedestrian Bridge connecting Millennium Park with Maggie Daley Park. October 2015.

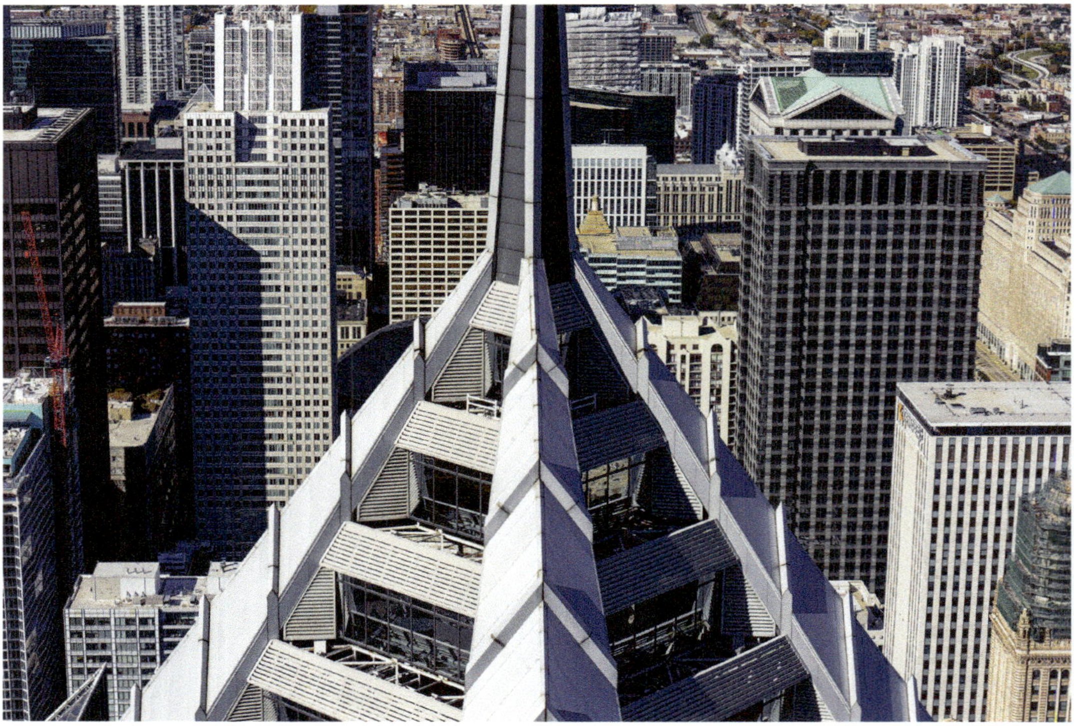

The top of Two Prudential Plaza (also known as Two Pru) in the Loop. October 2015.

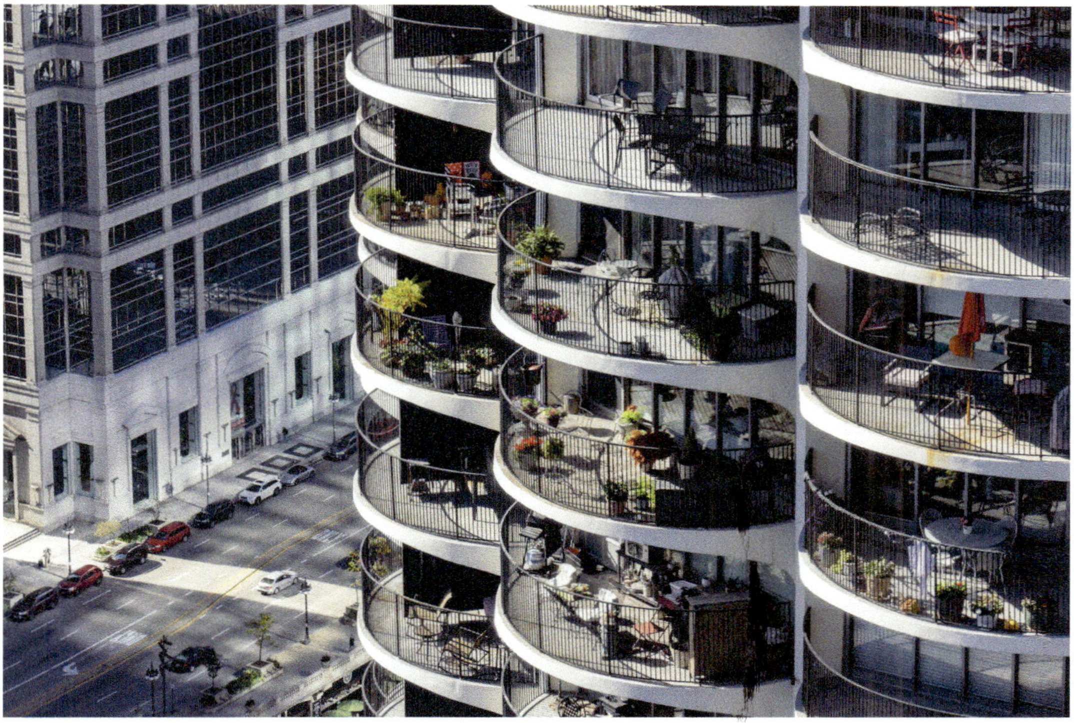

Marina City balconies. October 2024.

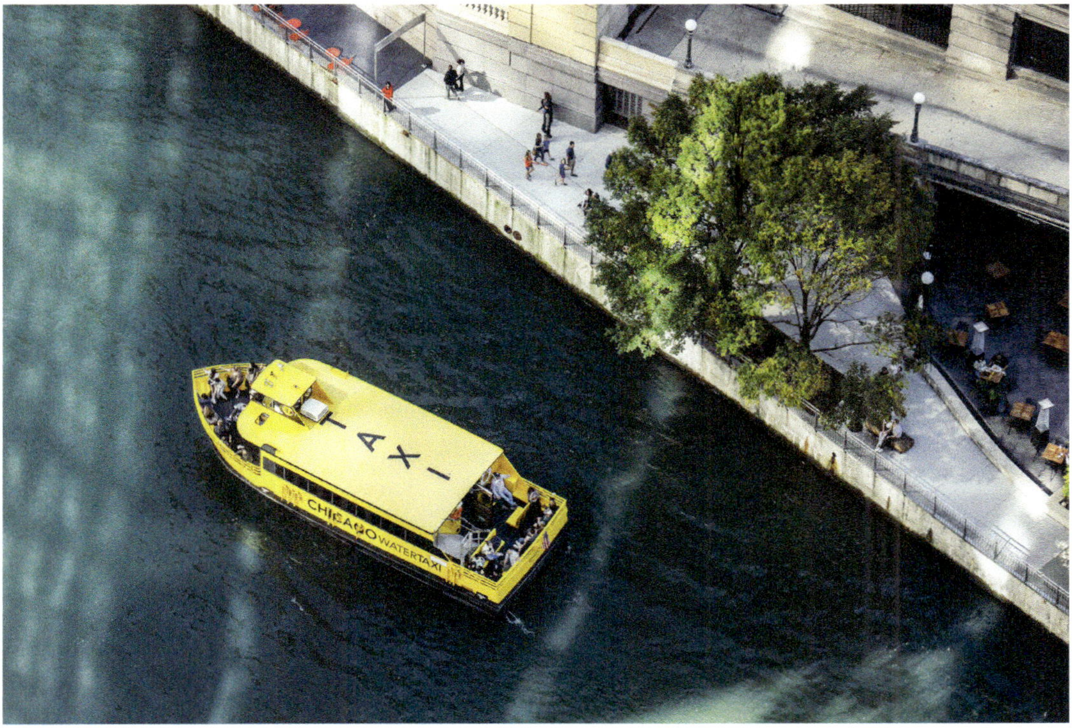

Water Taxi on the Main Stem of the Chicago River. October 2024.

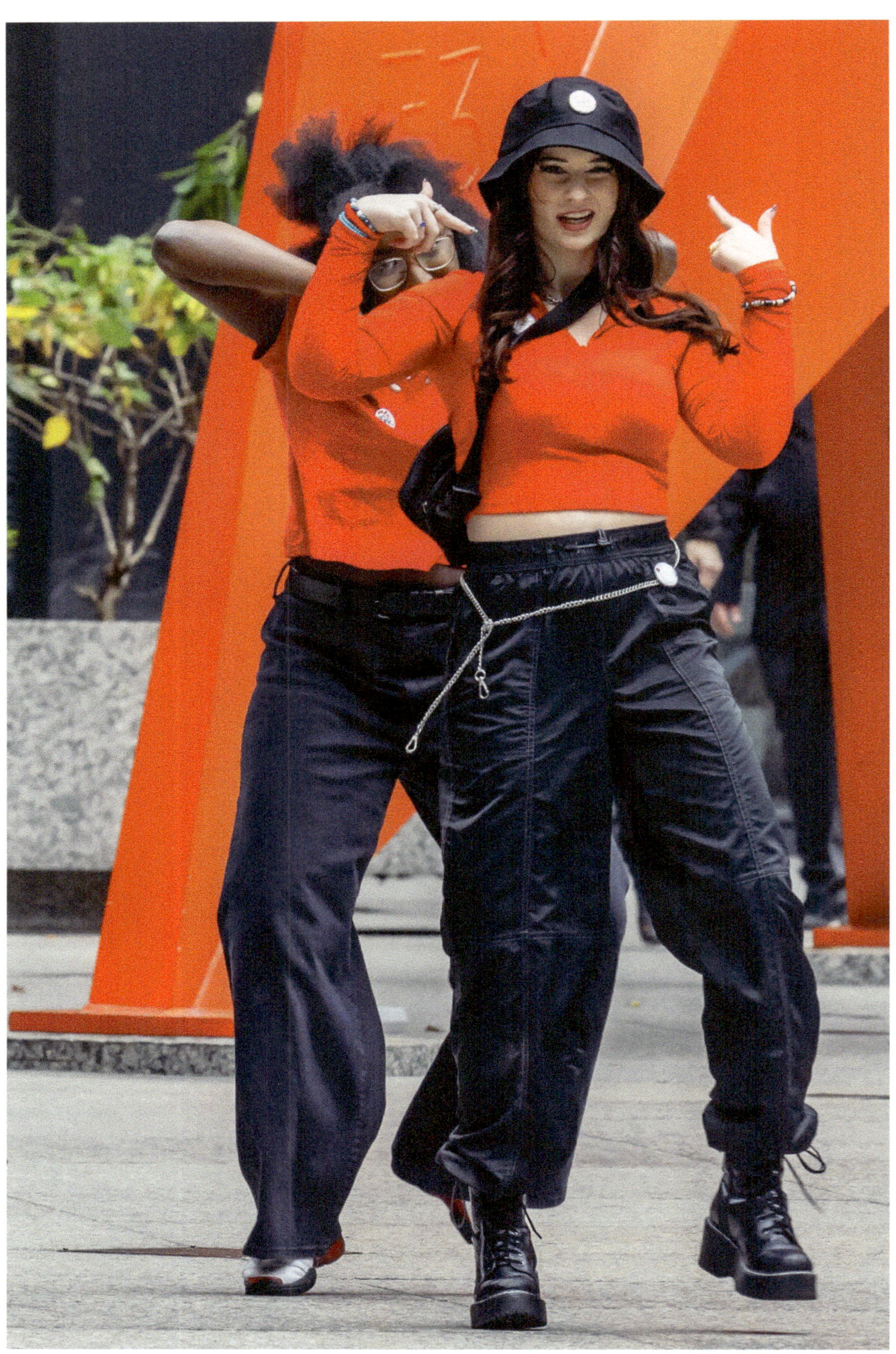

Federal Plaza. November 2024.

9
People

Of the 52 million people that visited Chicago in 2023, almost 2 million were from foreign parts. They came to a city that bustles with life. In the Loop there are buskers and vendors, businesspeople, tourists, theatergoers dressed for the occasion, and residents walking their dogs. You might see a Buddhist monk selling beads, hip-hop dancers in a plaza, Amish farmers that have come in on the train, or art students clutching their masterpieces. Millennium Park buzzes with activity, especially around Cloud Gate in the summer. Further south, Buckingham Fountain, the lakefront, and the Museum Campus have benches in convenient locations to relax, with or without a camera.

Beyond downtown, Chicago is a city of neighborhoods. According to the 2020 U.S. Census, 32% of the Chicago population are White, 30% Hispanic or Latino, 29% Black or African-American, and 7% Asian. Many neighborhoods are proud of their cultural identity. Several celebrate their heritage in annual parades. Notable examples are the Saint Patrick's Day parade and the Polish Constitution Day Parade in the Loop, and the Chinese Lunar New Year Parade in Chinatown. In addition to those with an ethnic flavor, there are other large parades in the Loop including those celebrating Memorial Day, Columbus Day, and Thanksgiving. Other crowd-inducing events include several summer festivals in Grant Park, and throughout the year, protests drawing attention to the issues of the day.

Photographer Tips

i) Some neighborhoods that are good for street photography, or just to hang out in, are Chinatown, Wicker Park, Old Town, Uptown, Logan Square, and Pilsen.
ii) If street photography feels awkward, annual parades offer entry-level opportunities. In the staging areas there will be interesting candid shots.

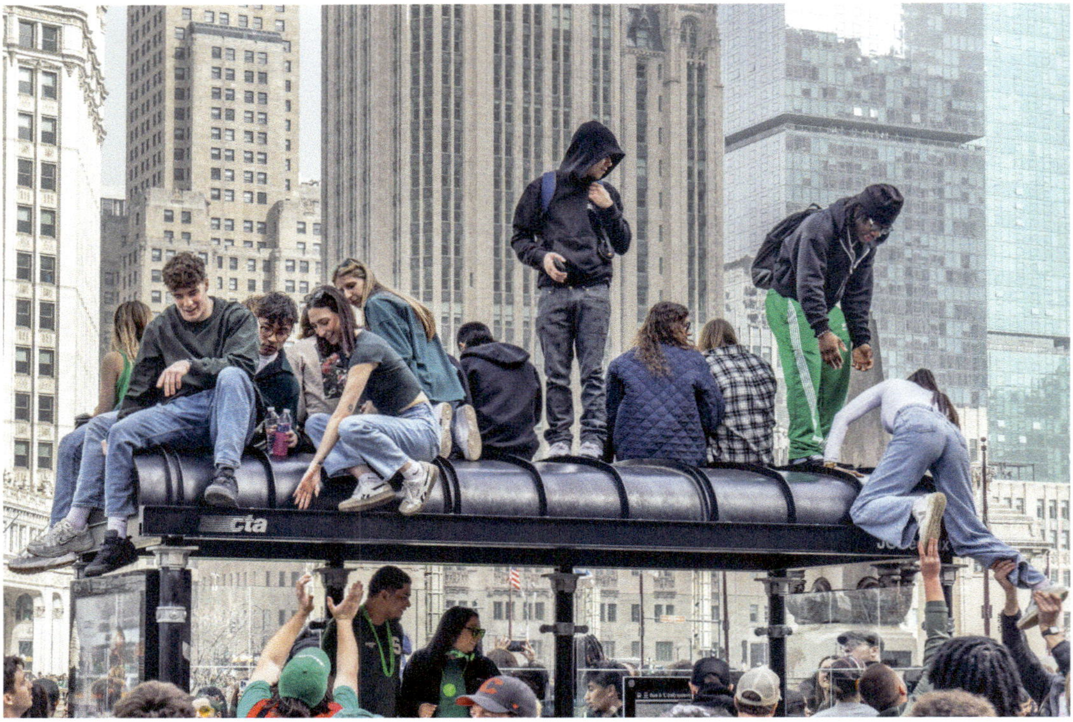

Wacker Drive. St. Patrick's Day celebrations. March 2025.

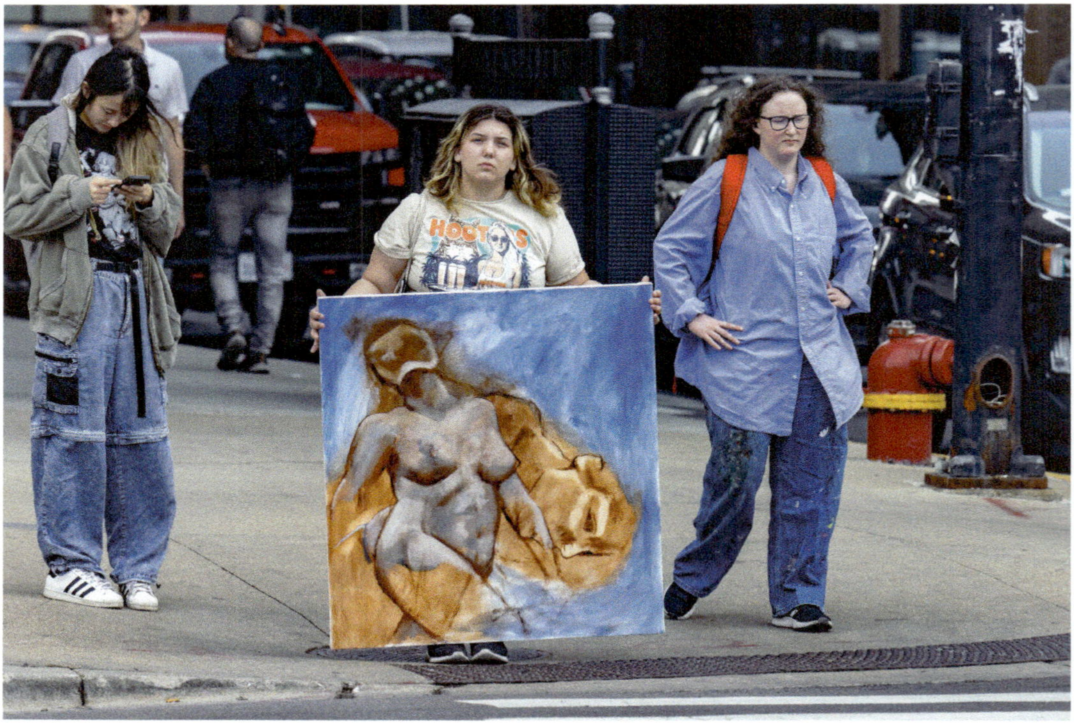

Michigan Avenue in the Loop. February 2024.

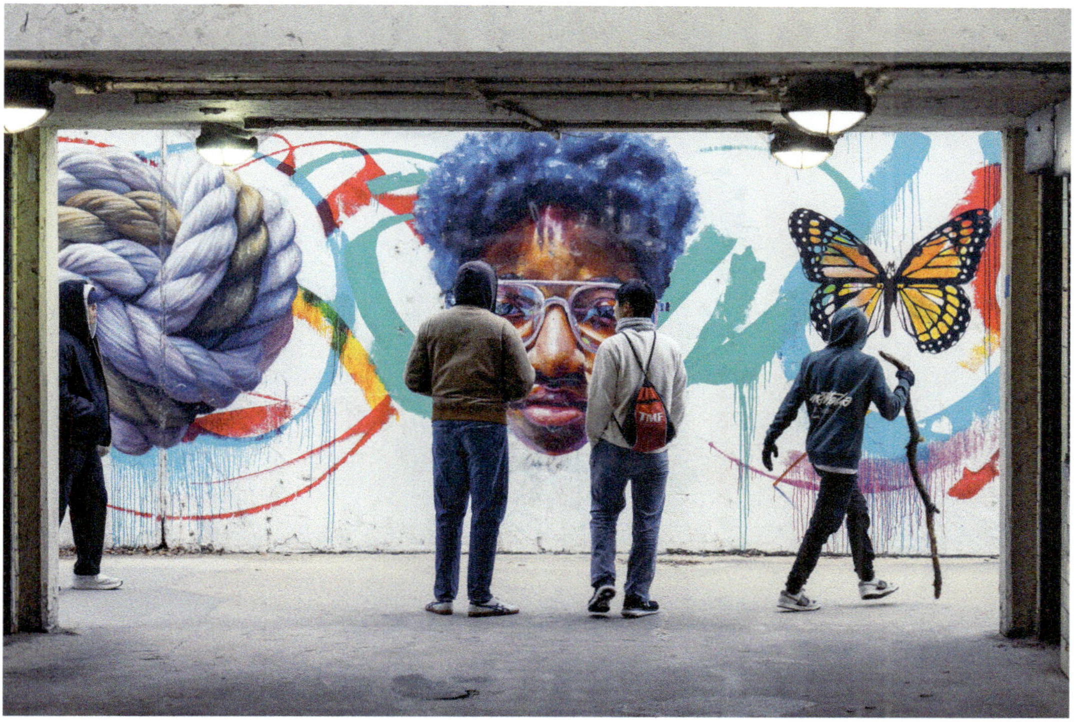

Oak Street Beach underpass. December 2024.

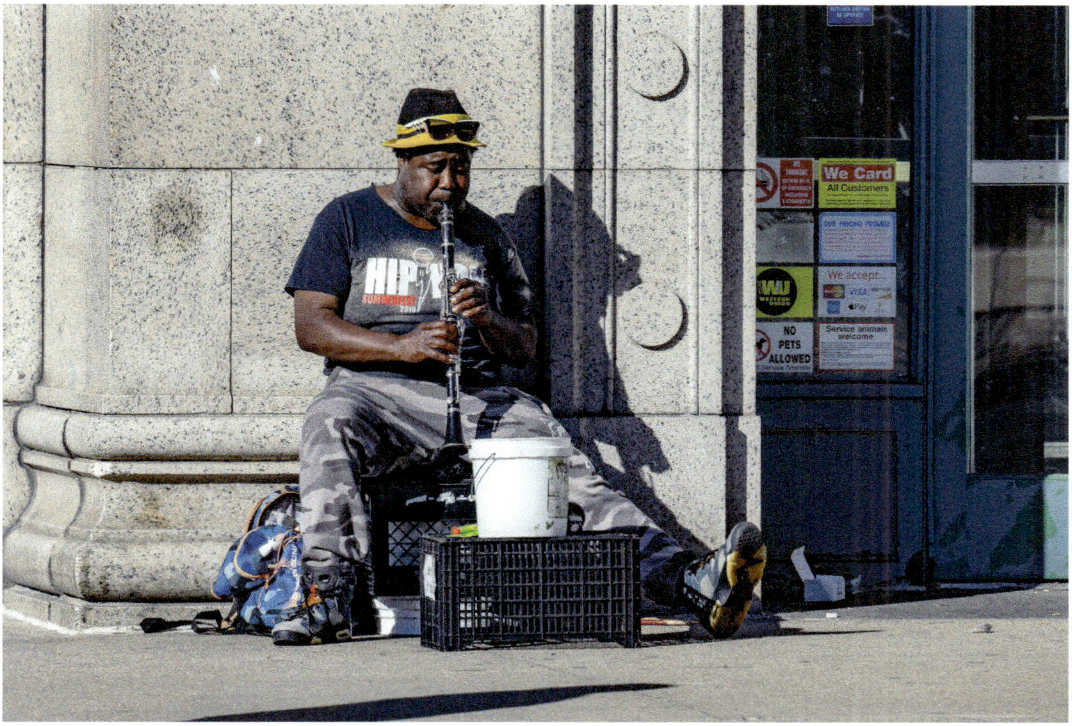

Michigan Avenue. October 2024.

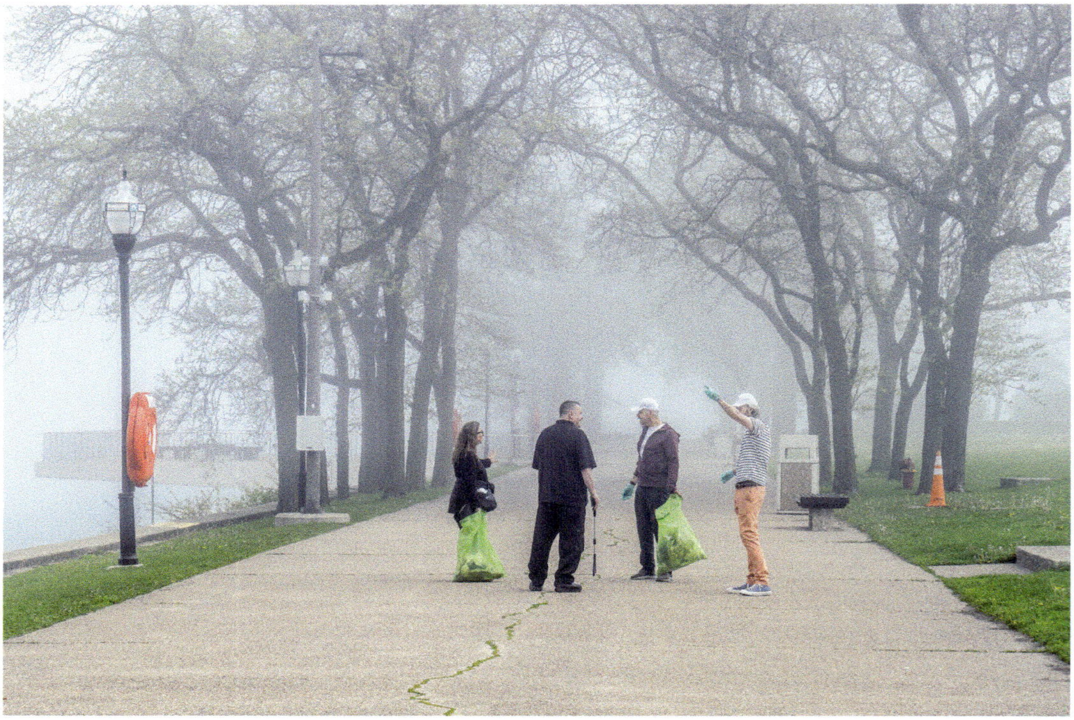

Volunteers cleaning up Olive Park. May 2025.

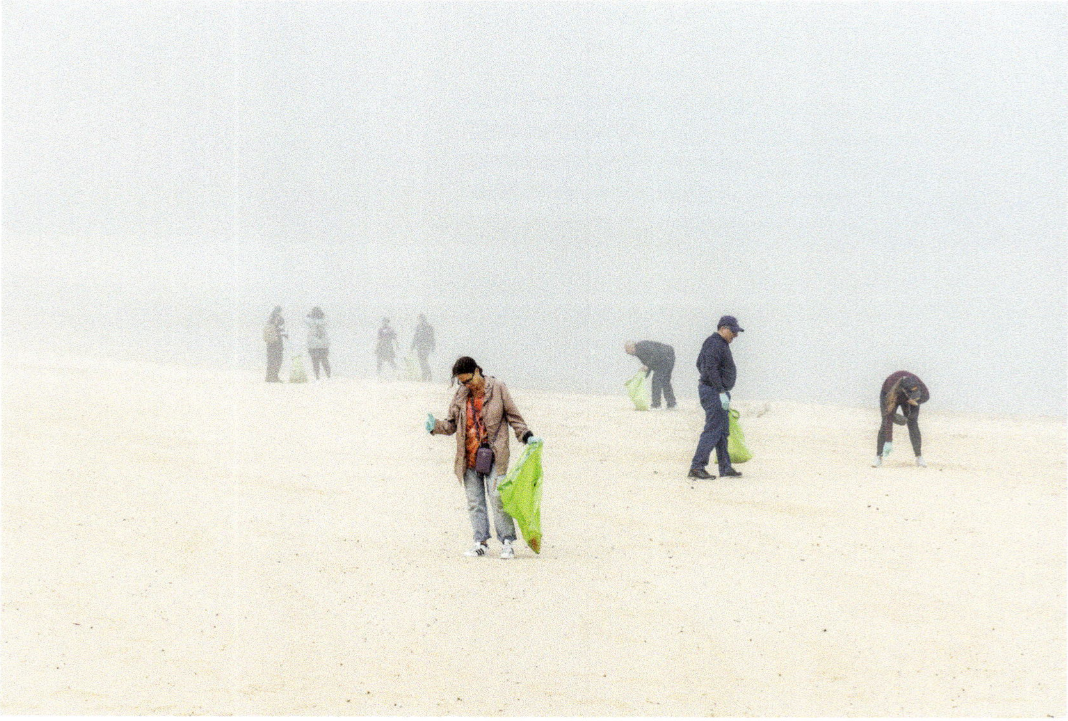

Volunteers cleaning up Ohio Street Beach. May 2025.

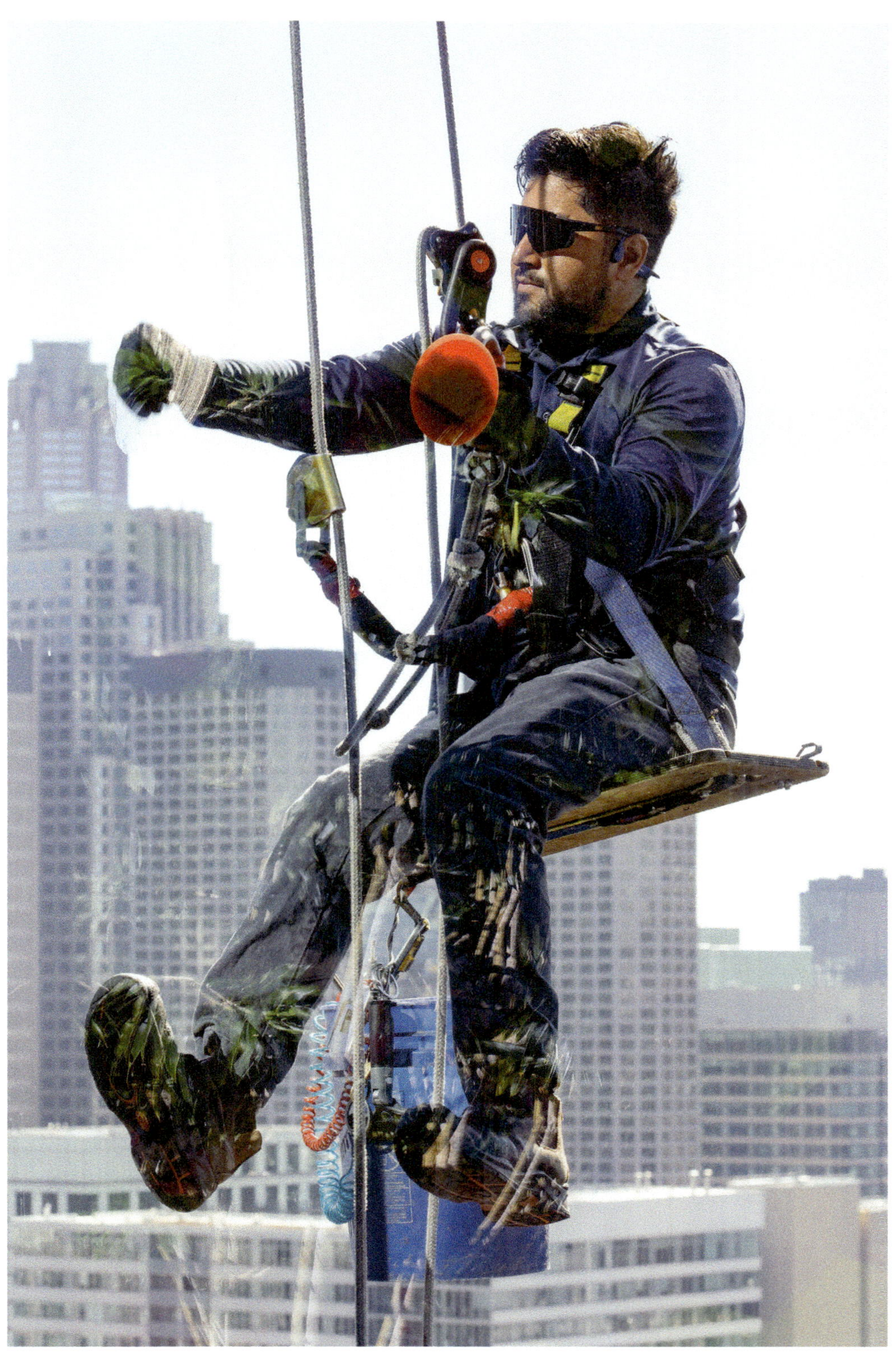

Window cleaner, Near West Side. October 2024.

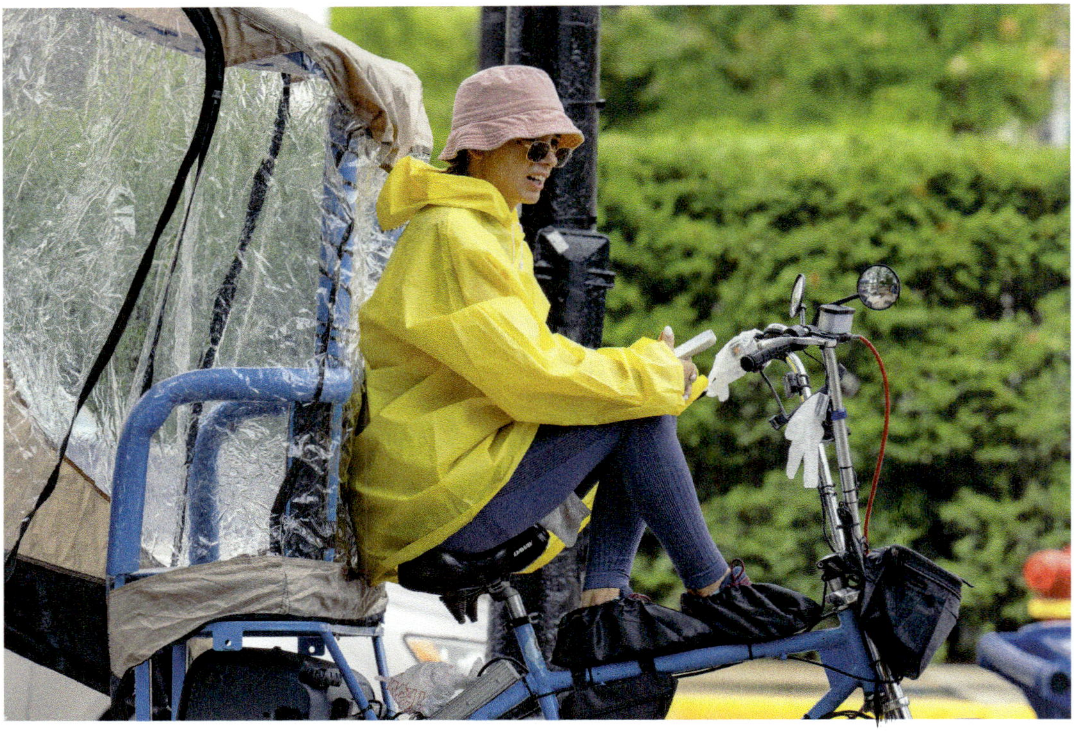

Columbus Drive in the Loop. August 2024.

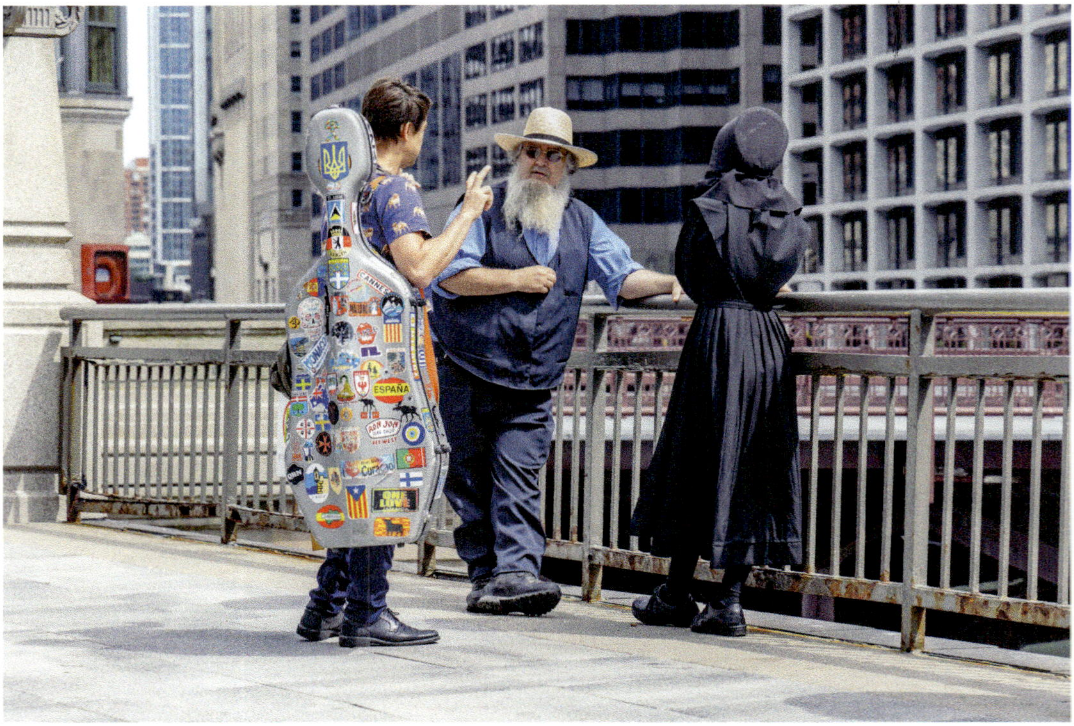

South Riverside Plaza. August 2022.

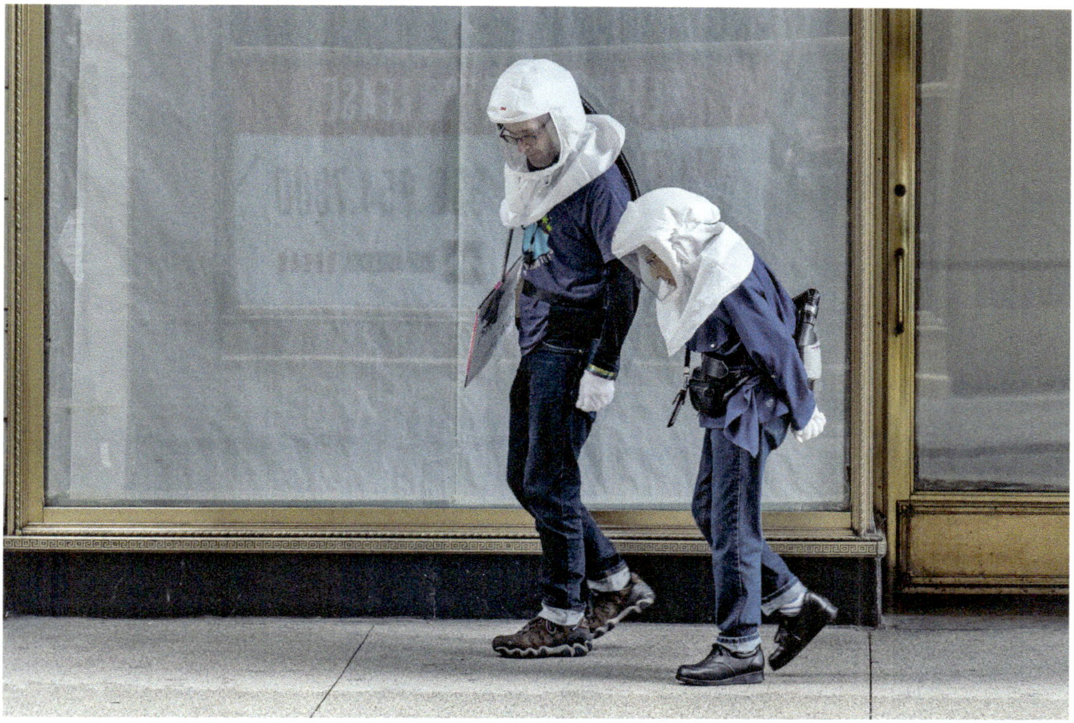

Jackson Boulevard in the Loop. June 2022.

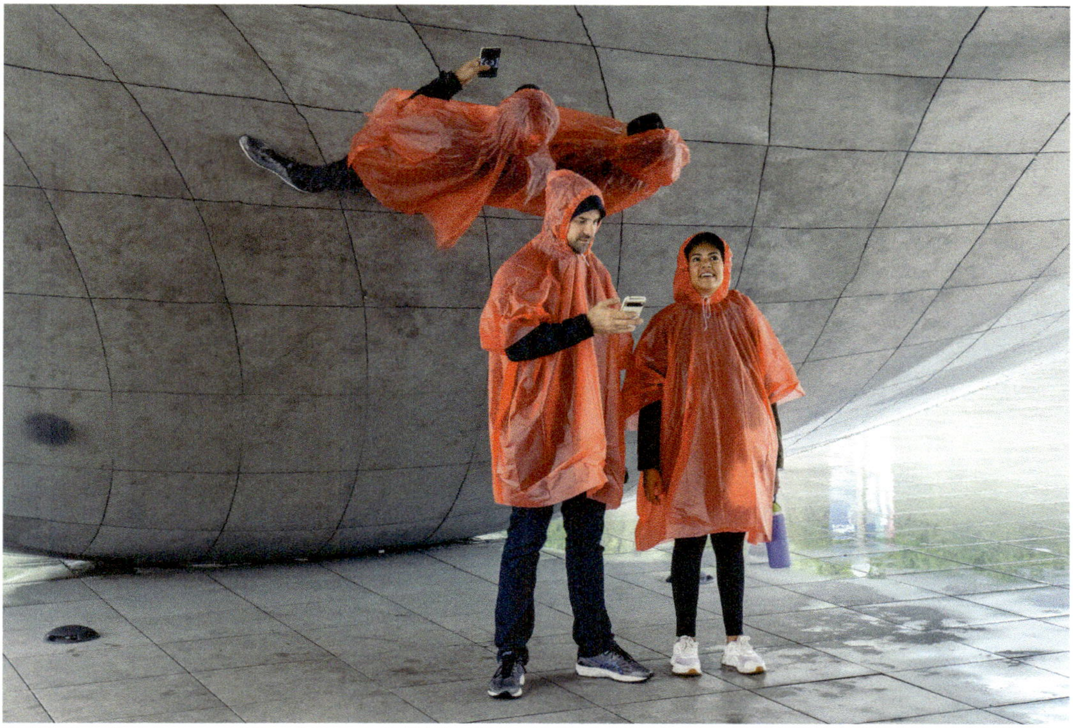

Cloud Gate. June 2025.

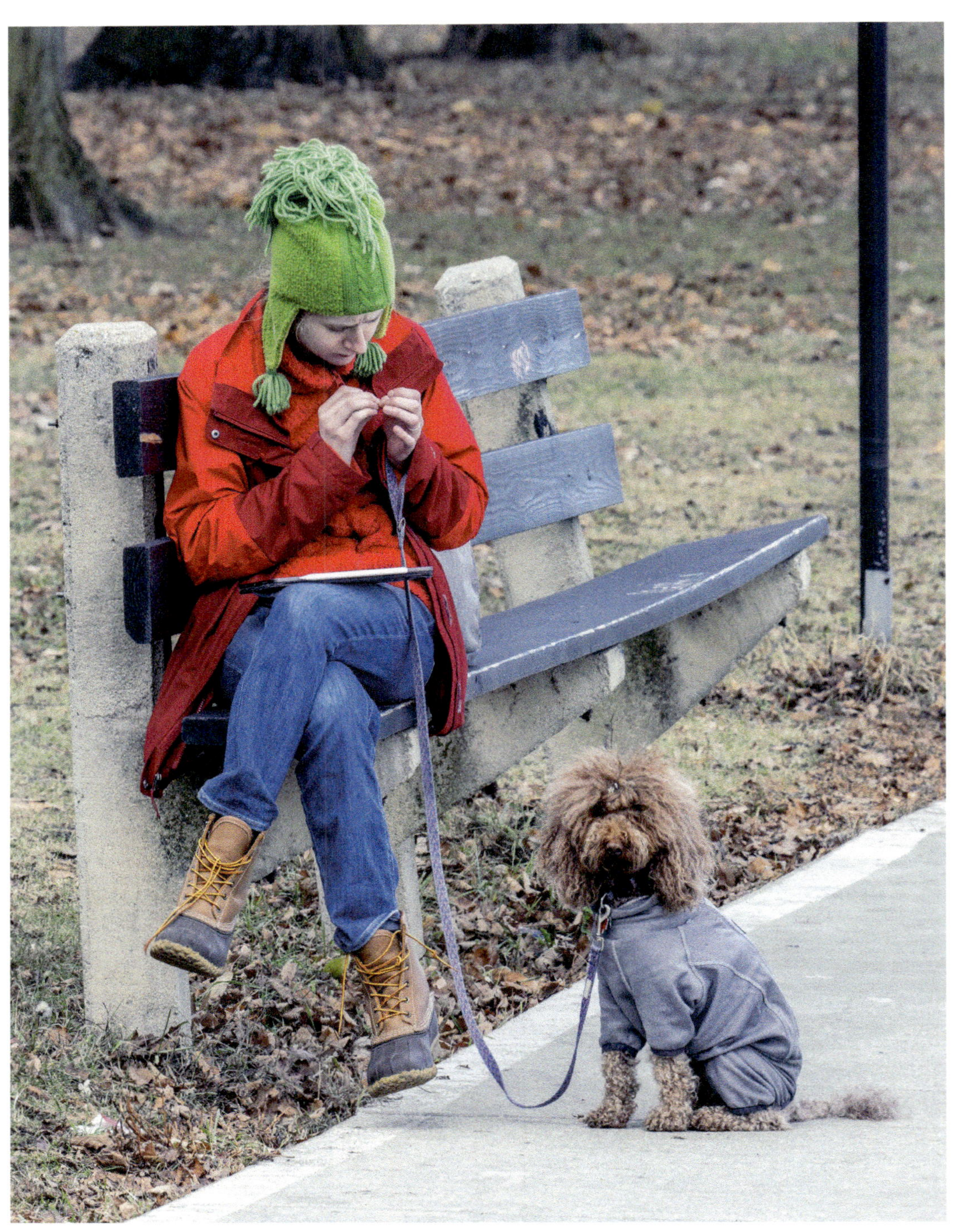

Belmont Harbor. December 2024.

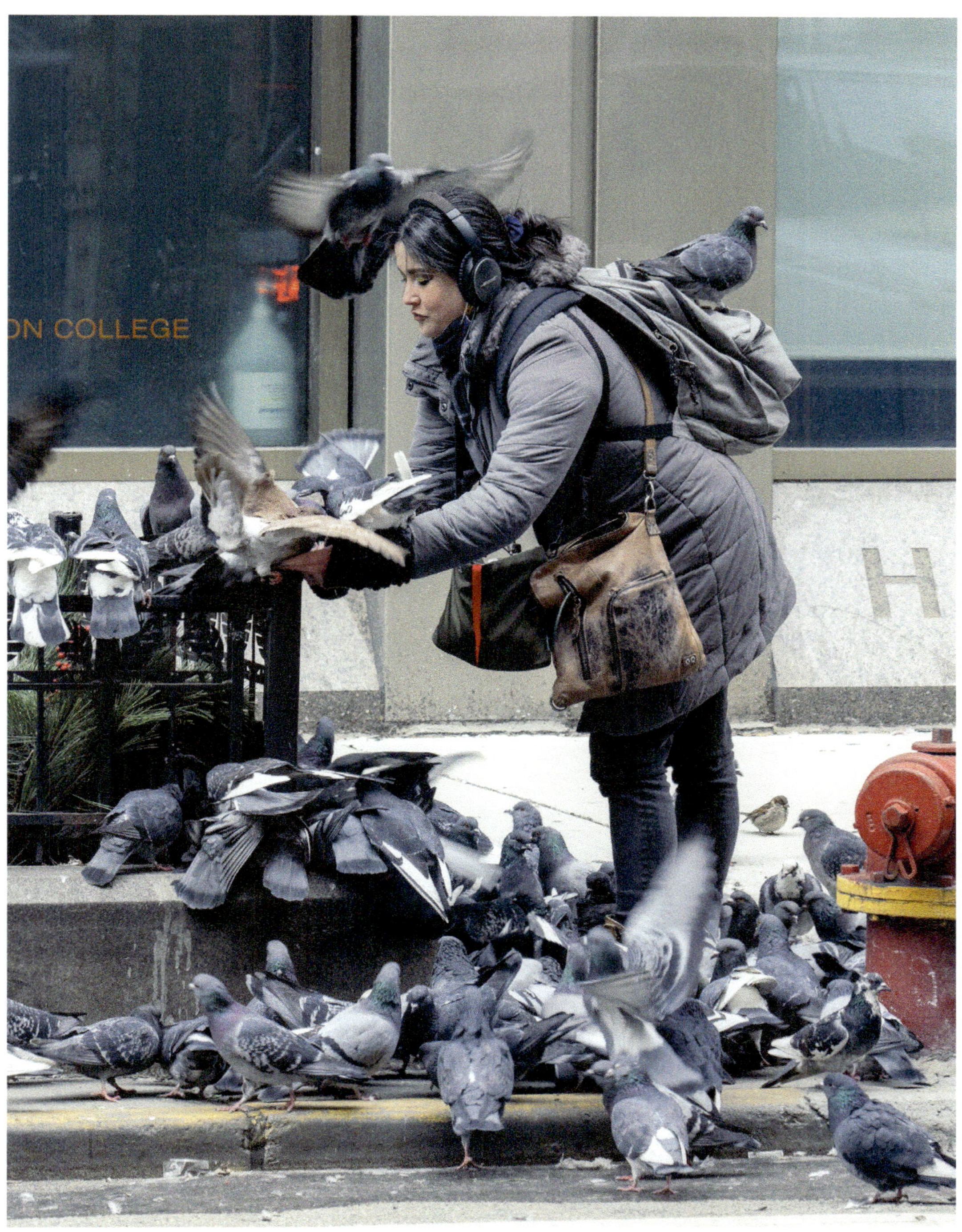

Lake Street. January 2025.

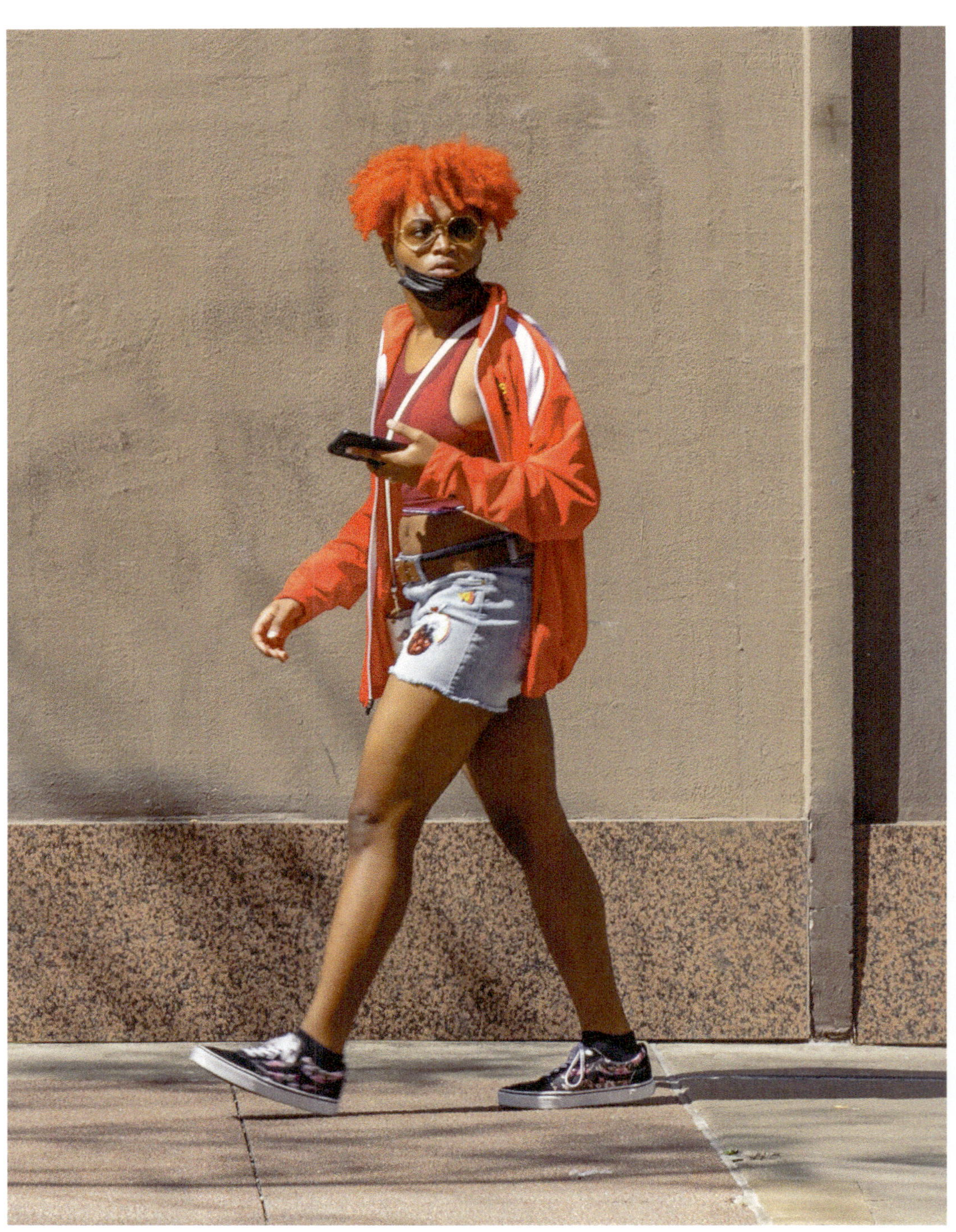

State Street. September 2022.

Afterword

There is a lot to see in Chicago and it's tempting to try to cover a lot of ground quickly, but it pays to slow down and look. If you are taking photographs, it's nice to capture those standard views but much more satisfying to see and capture something new. Photographer Robert Capa told us: "If your pictures aren't good enough, you're not close enough." My version of Capa's wisdom is: "If your pictures aren't good enough, you're walking too fast."

Although I have lived in Chicago for a decade, walking slowly I am still discovering new things. The city is not static. Old buildings are torn down or redeveloped and new ones constructed. New stores appear, old ones close or have a facelift, and there are different fashions and fads, and always lots of activity. In historian Dominic A. Pacyga's book, *Chicago: A Biography*, we are told: "In many ways Chicago is like a snake that sheds its skin every thirty years or so and puts on a new coat to conform to a new reality." If anything, in recent years the rate of change seems faster than "every thirty years." The photographs in this book can therefore only present a snapshot of Chicago at one point in time, a time in which downtown Chicago is an attractive place in which to live, work, or visit. For visitors, summer is the peak season but there are no off seasons. There are always things to see and do. The weather can be varied, but if it's raining or freezing, it's good to remember the old saying attributed to Ranulph Fiennes: "There's no such thing as bad weather, only inappropriate clothing." Whatever the weather, Chicago is a great city to see, with or without a camera.

Acknowledgments

I am indebted to Liz for carefully reading the manuscript and for many other things.

About the Author

Steve Geer is a scientist and photographer living in Chicago. He has exhibited photographs in more than thirty solo and group exhibitions in the U.S. and in Europe, has published his work in numerous photography magazines, and is on the board of directors of the Perspective Fine Art Photography Gallery in Evanston, IL. In 2019 Steve was a founding member of the P2 Collective, a group of photographers and poets producing an ekphrastic dialogue in which poems inspire photographs that then inspire further poems, and so on. Steve is a Fellow of the Royal Photographic Society (FRPS). To see more of his work, visit his website www.stevegeer.com.